Microsoft®

Works 3 For Windows™

Step by Step

PUBLISHED BY
Microsoft Press
A Division of Microsoft Corporation
One Microsoft Way
Redmond, Washington 98052-6399

Library of Congress Cataloging-in-Publication Data
Microsoft Works 3 for Windows step by step / ComputerPREP, Inc.
     p.   cm.
   Includes index.
   ISBN 1-55615-645-6
   1. Integrated software. 2. Microsoft Works for Windows.
I. ComputerPREP, Inc.
QA76.76.I57M52   1994
005.369--dc20   94-7234
                                    CIP

Printed and bound in the United States of America.

2 3 4 5 6 7 8 9 MLML 9 8 7 6 5

Distributed to the book trade in Canada by Macmillan of Canada, a division of Canada Publishing
Corporation.

A CIP catalogue record for this book is available from the British Library.

Microsoft Press books are available through booksellers and distributors worldwide. For further
information about international editions, contact your local Microsoft Corporation office. Or contact
Microsoft Press International directly at fax (206) 936-7329.

For ComputerPREP, Inc.
Project Manager: Kenneth Iversen
Managing Editor: Stephanie Karabets
Author: Tom Miller
Associate Editors: Jay Mann and Victoria Fodale

For Microsoft Press
Acquisitions Editor: Casey D. Doyle
Project Editor: Laura Sackerman

ComputerPREP & Microsoft Press

Microsoft Works 3 for Windows Step by Step has been created by the professional trainers and writers at ComputerPREP to the exacting standards you've come to expect from Microsoft Press. Together, we are pleased to present this self-paced training guide, which you can use individually or as part of a class.

ComputerPREP produces a variety of software training courseware for corporations, educational institutions, learning centers, and government agencies. ComputerPREP's three-phased training approach utilizes each student's previous knowledge to set learning expectations, introduces new software functions in easily understandable steps, and then helps apply evolved skills to real-world scenarios. *Microsoft Works 3 for Windows Step by Step* incorporates ComputerPREP's years of training experience to ensure that you'll receive the maximum return on your training time. You'll focus on the skills that increase productivity the most while working at your own pace and convenience.

Microsoft Press is the independent—and independent-minded—book publishing division of Microsoft Corporation. The leading publisher of information on Microsoft software, Microsoft Press is dedicated to providing the highest quality end-user training, reference, and technical books that make using Microsoft software easier, more enjoyable, and more productive.

After you've used this Step by Step book, please let us know what you think! Incorporating feedback from readers is a key component in continuously improving the books in the *Step by Step* series, and your help ensures that our materials remain as useful to you as possible.

Send your comments to:

Microsoft Press
Associate Publisher—Acquisitions
One Microsoft Way
Redmond, WA 98052-6399
Fax (206) 936-7329

WE'VE CHOSEN THIS SPECIAL LAY-FLAT BINDING

to make it easier for you to work through the step-by-step lessons while you're at your computer.

With little effort, you can make this book lie flat when you open it to any page. Simply press down on the inside (where the paper meets the binding) of any left-hand page, and the book will stay open to that page. You can open the book this way every time. The lay-flat binding will not weaken or crack over time.

It's tough, flexible, sturdy—and designed to last.

Contents

Part 1   Using the Word Processor

Part 4 Using Communications

Appendix

About This Book

Microsoft Works version 3 for Windows is an integrated software package that includes a word processor, a spreadsheet, a database, and a communications tool. Works also includes accessories that will help you work efficiently and creatively, such as a drawing application (Microsoft Draw), a graphics application (Clip Art), and an application for creating text objects with special effects (Word Art). Together, these features provide you with the tools necessary to accomplish almost any task.

Microsoft Works 3 for Windows Step by Step shows you how to efficiently use the most commonly used features of each Works productivity tool. You can use *Microsoft Works 3 for Windows Step by Step* as a self-paced tutorial or you can use it as a teaching aid in a classroom environment.

The disk located inside the back cover of this book contains files that you will use to complete hands-on exercises in each lesson. The "Getting Ready" section of this book has detailed instructions for copying these files to your computer's hard disk.

Finding the Best Starting Point

This book is designed primarily for people who are learning Microsoft Works for the first time. It is divided into four major parts, each dedicated to a different Works tool. The parts are written as sets of stand-alone exercises, so you can work through them independently.

- Part 1 introduces the Word Processor tool and shows you how to create, format, and enhance documents. You also learn how to use WorksWizards to create complex documents, such as form letters, and you create envelopes and mailing labels.

- Part 2 introduces the Spreadsheet tool. Topics in this part include how to create and modify spreadsheets and how to create charts.

- Part 3 introduces the Database tool and shows you how to create, modify, and query databases, and how to use the database reporting feature.

- Part 4 introduces the Communications tool. In this part, you learn how to connect to computer bulletin boards, online information services, and other computers by using a modem. You also find out how to send and receive information and how to record and play back scripts.

The lessons in each part progress in complexity. The first lesson in each part presents basic concepts and helps you to become comfortable with the tool being used. The lessons that follow cover more complex concepts and methods for using the tool to its full potential and applying it to your own work.

Every lesson contains a lesson summary near the end, which you can use to decide if you need to work through a lesson. If topics are discussed that you don't know about already, you can work through the sections of the lesson that pertain to those topics. If many of the topics are unfamiliar, you might want to work through the entire lesson.

If you are new to Microsoft Works, or to computers in general, you might want to start with Lesson 1 and progress through the lessons sequentially. If you are familiar with Works, or if you want to learn about a particular Works tool, you might decide to start with the part that covers the tool you want to learn about first.

The following table can help you choose an appropriate starting point.

If you are	Follow these steps
New to using a computer or to using Microsoft Windows	Read the "Getting Ready" section of this book and follow the instructions for copying the practice files to your computer's hard disk. Pay special attention to the sections "If You Are New to Microsoft Windows" and "If You Are New to Using a Mouse." Next, work through the parts of the book in any order, but work through the lessons in each part in numerical order.
Familiar with using Microsoft Windows, but new to using Microsoft Works	Read the "Getting Ready" section of this book and copy the practice files to your computer's hard disk. Next, work through the parts of the book in any order, but work through the lessons in each part in numerical order.
Familiar with using word processor, spreadsheet, database, or communications applications.	Follow the instructions in the "Getting Ready" section of this book to copy the practice files to your computer's hard disk. Next, find the part of the book that covers the tool you want to learn about, and then work through the lessons in that part in any order.
Experienced with Microsoft Works	Read the "Getting Ready" section of this book and copy the practice files to your computer's hard disk. Next, you may want to work through lessons 3 and 8, which step you through the process for using two new Works features: WorksWizards and templates. Work through the rest of the lessons in any order.

Using This Book as a Classroom Aid

If you are an instructor, you can use *Microsoft Works 3 for Windows Step by Step* as a classroom aid while teaching your course. You might want to use selected lessons as a supplement to your own curriculum or you can use this book as a complete training manual.

If you choose to teach all of the lessons in this book, you will probably need to allocate two days of classroom time to adequately present the lessons, answer questions, and incorporate any customized exercises.

Conventions Used in This Book

To ensure that your learning is optimized, it is important that you understand the terms and conventions used in this book before you begin any of the lessons.

Procedural Conventions

- Each exercise is presented as a series of consecutively numbered steps, beginning with the number 1. A triangular bullet (▶) indicates that an exercise contains only one step.

- The word "choose" is used when you are to execute a command from a menu or a dialog box.

- The word "select" is used when you are to highlight directories, filenames, or text boxes, and when you are to select options in a dialog box.

- The words "turn on" and "turn off" are used when you are to activate or deactivate a check box option in a dialog box.

Notational Conventions

- Text that you need to type appears in bold lowercase type; for example, "Type **income analysis**"

- Important terms appear in italic type when they are first defined; for example, "A *header* is information that prints at the top of every document page."

- Filenames, directory names, and directory paths appear in uppercase type unless you are being instructed to type them; for example, "Open the WORKSSBS directory."

Keyboard Conventions

- Names of keys that you are to press appear in small capital letters; for example, "Press TAB."

- When a plus sign (+) appears between two or more key names, you are to press the keys at the same time. For example, "Press SHIFT+TAB" means that you should hold down the SHIFT key while pressing the TAB key.

- When a comma (,) appears between two or more key names, you are to press each of the keys consecutively rather than together. For example, "Press ALT, F, O" means that you should press and release the ALT key, press and release the F key, and then press and release the O key.

Other Features of This Book

- Text in the left margin provides additional information or directs you to other sections in this book or in your Microsoft Works 3 for Windows documentation.

- The One Step Further exercises that appear at the end of each lesson explore additional techniques or options related to the skills you learned in the lesson.

- Each lesson contains a lesson summary that lists the skills you have learned in the lesson and briefly reviews how to accomplish particular tasks.

- The Review & Practice exercises at the end of each part of the book reinforce the skill you have learned in that part.

- Each Works tool contains a toolbar with buttons you can click to execute many commonly used commands. If you are instructed to click a button, you will see a picture of that button in the left margin.

- The Appendix, "Matching the Exercises," shows you the options and settings used in this book. If your screens do not match the illustrations shown in the lesson exercises, or if your exercise results are different than those presented in the book, you can refer to this appendix to see if your settings or options need to be changed.

Cross-References to Microsoft Works Documentation

At the end of every lesson is a table listing the topics covered and where to find related information in your Microsoft Works documentation. Some marginal notes in the lesson will also direct you to your documentation for additional information.

Online Help

Microsoft Works contains a Help system that serves as a complete online reference tool. In the Help system you will find information about all of the Works features and how to use them. In the "Getting Ready" section of this book you will tour the online Help system.

At the end of each lesson you will find a table of online Help references for each of the major features presented in the lesson.

Microsoft Works User's Guide

The *Microsoft Works User's Guide* that comes with your Works software guides you through the procedures necessary to install, set up, and start Works. It also explains application features, how to use each of the features, and how to access the Help system.

Getting Ready

This section tells you how to install the practice files that come with this book. It also helps you become comfortable with the basic skills required to start using Microsoft Works and reviews some fundamental Windows concepts.

You will learn how to:

- Install the practice files on your hard drive.
- Start Microsoft Windows.
- Start Microsoft Works.
- Explore the window, menu, and dialog box components of Microsoft Windows.
- Obtain online help in Microsoft Works.

Installing the Practice Files

If you've never used a mouse, read the section "If You Are New to Using a Mouse" before you install the practice files.

The practice files you'll use with this book are designed to teach you efficient methods for using Works effectively. Although your needs may require you to use Works in ways other than those depicted in this book, the practice files cover frequently used tasks that you are likely to encounter in your own work.

All of the practice files you'll use with this book are contained on a disk named "Practice Files for Microsoft Works 3 for Windows Step by Step," located inside the back cover. Before you can complete the exercises in the book, you'll need to copy the practice files to your hard drive. There is a special program on the practice files disk that completes this process for you.

Copy the practice files to your hard drive

1 Turn on your computer and insert the practice files disk in either drive A or drive B.

2 If Windows is already running, open the Program Manager and choose Run from the File menu. If Windows is not running, go to step 4.

3 In the Command Line box, type **a:\install** (or **b:\install**, depending on which drive contains the practice files disk), click the OK button, and go to step 5.

Note Do not type a space between the colon (:) and the backslash (\).

4 To copy the practice files to your hard drive using MS-DOS, type **a:\install** (or **b:\install**) at the MS-DOS prompt (usually C:\> or something similar) and then press ENTER.

5 Follow the instructions that appear on screen to complete the installation process.

A special program on the practice files disk copies the files to your hard drive and places them in the WORKSSBS subdirectory of the Microsoft Works for Windows home directory. You'll access the WORKSSBS subdirectory whenever you open a practice file.

Lesson Background

The exercises used in this book are based on the following scenario: You work in the video department of a company named West Coast Sales and have just been promoted to the department manager position. Your first task is to coordinate an inventory reduction sale. Your responsibilities include advertising the sale, tracking sales trends, monitoring inventory before and during the sale, and electronically sharing your information with other West Coast Sales affiliates. The previous department manager used Works for Windows to accomplish all of these tasks. Before you can assume your new responsibilities, you need to learn how to use Works. The practice files you just installed contain some of the previous department manager's files. You'll use these files as you learn to use Works.

Starting Microsoft Windows and Microsoft Works

The following procedures show you how to start Windows, if it is not already running, and how to start Works. Depending on how your computer is set up, your screen may look different than the screens shown in the following illustrations. For more information about Windows, see the *Microsoft Windows User's Guide*.

Start Windows

If Windows is not already running, you can start it from the MS-DOS command prompt.

▶ At the MS-DOS command prompt, type **win** and press ENTER.

Your Program Manager window should now resemble the following illustration. The Program Manager window is a central location from which you can start any of the Windows-based applications on your computer.

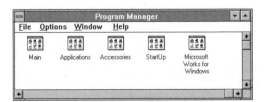

Regardless of what application you're using, there are some elements that are common to all Windows screens. Everything that appears on your screen constitutes your *desktop*. Desktop information appears in *windows*, which are individual work areas framed by borders. You can change the size and location of any window on your desktop. You can also open multiple windows simultaneously and move or copy information between them.

An *icon* is a named symbol that represents an application or a document. Your Program Manager window contains icons arranged in *program groups*. These program groups usually contain all the programs associated with a particular application.

Start Works

Microsoft
Works for
Windows

Microsoft
Works

1 In the Program Manager window, double-click the Microsoft Works For Windows icon.

The Microsoft Works For Windows program group window opens.

2 Double-click the Microsoft Works icon.

The Startup dialog box appears.

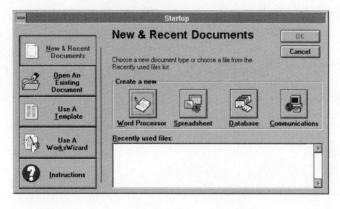

The Startup dialog box is a control center from which you access files, productivity tools, and accessories.

Note   If the Welcome To Microsoft Works screen appears instead of the Startup dialog box, click the Skip Welcome Screen button to prevent the screen from appearing each time you start Works. If you want to return to the welcome screen, you can access it from the Help menu.

If You Are New to Microsoft Windows

If you are a new Microsoft Windows user you will find it helpful to have a general idea of how Windows operates. Windows is an operating environment in which you can run multiple applications simultaneously and share text, data, and graphics between applications. This information sharing is possible because Windows provides a common interface for different application programs, allowing them to all operate in the same way.

You should become familiar with the basic elements of Microsoft Windows before you proceed with the exercises presented in this book. Once you understand these elements, you will find it easy to understand and use any Windows-based application.

Using Window Components

Although all Windows-based applications do not look exactly the same, they do share the common window components shown in the following illustration.

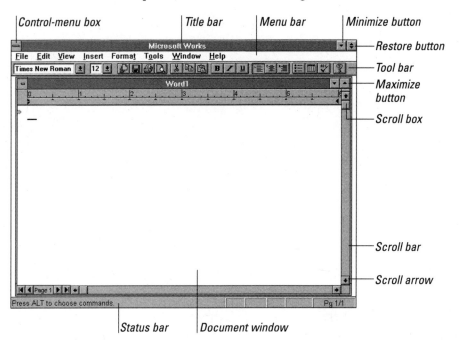

You access window components with the mouse to move, size, scroll through, and close a window.

To	Do this
Scroll through a window	Click a scroll bar or drag a scroll box.
Change the size of a window	Drag any edge of the window.

To	Do this
Enlarge a window to fill the entire screen	Click the Maximize button.
Reduce a window to an icon	Click the Minimize button.
Restore a window to its previous size	Click the Restore button.
Move a window	Drag the window's title bar.
Close a window	Double-click the Control-menu box.

Using Windows in Microsoft Works

In Works, each document, spreadsheet, or database opens within a window. You can have multiple windows open at the same time and switch between them by clicking the title bar of the window you want to work in or by using the Window menu.

Using Menus

Microsoft Works commands appear within menus that you access from the *menu bar*, which is located above the toolbar. You can choose commands from the menu bar using the mouse or the keyboard. To choose a command using the mouse, you click a menu name in the menu bar. When the corresponding menu opens, you click the command you want to execute.

The following illustration shows the File menu opened from the menu bar.

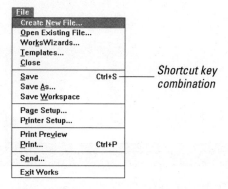

To the right of some command names you will see a *shortcut key* combination, which denotes the keys you can press while working in a document window to activate that command without using the menu system. Shortcut key combinations can save you time and are useful when you have to type large amounts of text and don't want to take your hands away from the keyboard.

If you are not using a mouse, you can choose commands from the menu bar by using the keyboard. Every menu name has a keyboard equivalent that you can use by holding down ALT and pressing the key that corresponds to the underlined character in the menu name. After a menu is open, you can execute a command from the keyboard by pressing the key that corresponds to the underlined character in the command name. For example, to open the File menu in the Works Word Processor, you would hold down ALT and type **F** on the keyboard. After the File menu opens, you would type **S** to choose the Save command.

Not all available commands will be appropriate for the operations you are performing. Commands that do not apply to your current situation are not accessible and appear dimmed on the menu. For example, the Paste command on the Edit menu will appear dimmed until you choose either the Cut or the Copy command.

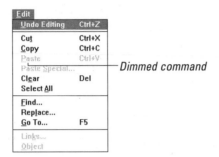

— *Dimmed command*

A check mark displayed to the left of a command indicates that the command is already in effect. For example, the check mark to the left of the Ruler command in the following illustration means that the ruler will appear on your screen.

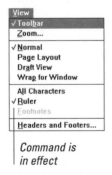

*Command is
in effect*

If you want to close a menu without choosing a command, you can click the menu name or press ESC.

Using Dialog Boxes

Many menu commands are followed by an ellipsis (...), which indicates that a *dialog box* appears when you choose that command. A dialog box appears because additional information is necessary to execute the chosen command. To supply the needed information, you may have to type text or numbers or make selections from groups of options.

You can change typed information or select different options before you execute the command. When you are certain that you have correctly specified the options you want, you execute the command by clicking the OK button or pressing ENTER. If you want to close a dialog box without executing a command, you click the Cancel button or press ESC.

Controls are the components of a dialog box that you use to supply the information needed to execute the command. All dialog boxes contain at least one of the controls shown in the following illustration.

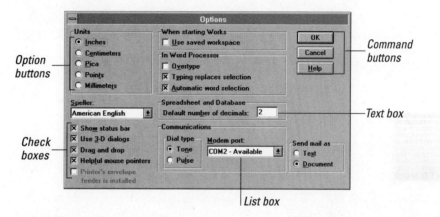

Option buttons   You use an option button to select a single option from a set of two or more options. A black dot appears in the center of an option button when it is selected. In the Options dialog box, the currently selected unit of measurement is inches. If you want to change the unit of measurement from inches to centimeters, you can select the Centimeters option button.

Check boxes   You use a check box to turn an option on or off. When you turn on a check box option, an *x* appears in the box.

List boxes   A list box shows the choices that are available for an option. If the list is too long to be displayed fully in the box, you can use the scroll bar in the list box or you can click the down-arrow button to view the hidden part of the list.

Text boxes   You type text or numbers in a text box. For example, in the Options dialog box, you can type a number in the Default Number Of Decimals text box to specify the number of decimals that will be assigned to numeric entries in spreadsheet or database documents. Sometimes there will already be text in a text box when a dialog box appears. You can accept the information that is already there or type new text.

Command buttons   You choose a command button to complete an operation or to display additional options. A command button name followed by an ellipsis indicates that more options are available in the form of another dialog box. If a command button appears dimmed, it is not appropriate for the choices you have specified, and it is not available.

Tabs   You use tabs to view additional sections of a dialog box. The illustration on the next page shows a dialog box with tabs.

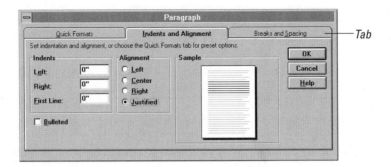

Tab

Selecting Dialog Box Options

You don't have to move through dialog box options in any particular order or direction. You can use the mouse to click any dialog box item. If you are not using a mouse, you can press TAB to move from option to option, or you can hold down ALT and press the key corresponding to the underlined letter in an option name.

The following table describes how to use the mouse to select dialog box options.

To	Do this
Select an option button	Click the option button.
Deselect an option button	Click another option button.
Turn a check box on or off	Click the check box.
Select an item in a list	Click the item.
Move to a text box	Click the text box.
Select text in a text box	Double-click to select a word or drag the mouse to select a group of words.
Scroll through a list	Click the scroll bars or scroll boxes.
Select a tab	Click the tab.

Using Toolbars

Toolbars contain buttons that provide shortcuts for executing commands. For example, instead of choosing the Print command from the File menu to print a document, you can click the Print button on the toolbar.

In Works, there is a toolbar for each productivity tool, located below the menu bar. The Word Processor toolbar is shown in the following illustration.

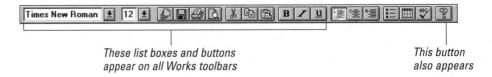

These list boxes and buttons appear on all Works toolbars

This button also appears

When you position the mouse pointer over a toolbar button, a descriptive label appears to identify the function of the button. Toolbars provide the quickest method for accomplishing most Works operations, so you'll be using the toolbar frequently as you complete the exercises in this book.

If You Are New to Using a Mouse

Many features of Microsoft Works and other Windows-based applications, such as menu bars, toolbars, and dialog boxes, are designed primarily for mouse use. You can perform most tasks in Works using the keyboard; however, using the mouse to accomplish these tasks is often easier and faster than using the keyboard.

Mouse Pointers

When you use a mouse, you move an on-screen symbol called a *pointer*. The pointer indicates the position in your document at which the next action will occur. To move the pointer, you slide the mouse across a flat surface or a mouse pad in the direction you want the pointer to move. Should you run out of room to move the mouse, you can pick it up and put it down again. As long as you don't click a mouse button, lifting and repositioning the mouse will not affect your document in any way.

As you perform different actions and drag the pointer across different parts of a Works document window, the shape of the pointer changes. As you become familiar with Works, you will recognize each of the varying pointer shapes as an indicator of what action you can execute at that point. As you work through the exercises in this book, you will use the following pointers.

This pointer	Appears when you point to
▹	A title bar to move a window, the menu bar or the toolbar to choose a command or click a button, or a scroll bar to scroll through a document.
I	Text in a text document, a cell, or the formula bar in a spreadsheet or database document. If you click text, a blinking vertical bar called the *insertion point* appears.
✚	A spreadsheet cell or database field.
DRAG MOVE COPY	Highlighted text. If you drag the highlighted text, the DRAG pointer changes to the MOVE pointer. If you hold down CTRL while dragging highlighted text, the DRAG pointer changes to the COPY pointer.
⌕ ZOOM	Text in the Print Preview window. Use this pointer to magnify the view of your document.

This pointer	Appears when you point to
⇥⏸⏪ ADJUST ⬍ ADJUST	A column heading or row heading boundary in a spreadsheet or database document to change the column width or row height.
☝	A Help topic term that you can click to display another topic.

Using the Mouse

There are four basic mouse actions that you will use as you work through this book.

Point   Position the mouse pointer over an item.

Click   Point to an item and quickly press and release the mouse button. You click to move around a document or to select an item on the screen.

Double-click   Point to an item and press and release the mouse button twice in rapid succession. Double-clicking is a shortcut for many Works tasks.

Drag   Hold down the mouse button while you move the mouse. You can drag to highlight data in a text document or to highlight a range of spreadsheet cells or database fields.

Unless you are instructed otherwise, use the left mouse button to click, double-click, and drag.

Using Help

The Works Help system contains a window with information about how to use Help. To access this information, choose How To Use Help from the Help menu.

Occasionally, you may forget how to perform a certain task or how to use a specific tool. To help keep you on track, Works provides an extensive online Help system. You can access Help information about the current task you are performing or you can search for specific information.

Use Help Contents

The Help Contents screen is a list of main Help topics that guide you to other areas of the Help system.

1   Click the Cancel button in the Startup dialog box.

The dialog box closes.

2   From the Help menu, choose Contents.

The Help Contents screen appears, as shown in the following illustration.

Notice the topics that appear with a solid underline. When you click a topic with a solid underline, a different Help screen appears with information about the topic.

3 Click the topic "Works for Windows Basic Skills."

The "Works for Windows Basic Skills" topic expands and its subtopics appear.

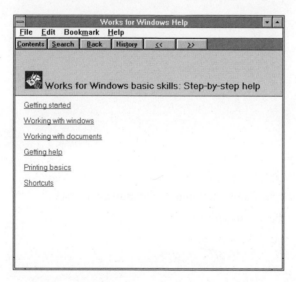

Pointing hand pointer

The pointer changes to the shape of a pointing hand when you place it on an underlined topic.

4 Click the topic "Working with documents," and then click the topic "Creating a document."

A Help screen of information about the "Creating a document" topic appears.

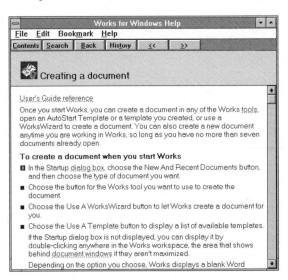

Notice the terms that appear with a dotted underline. When you click a term with a dotted underline, a glossary definition appears in a small pop-up window.

5 Click the term "dialog box."

A pop-up window appears with the glossary definition of the term "dialog box."

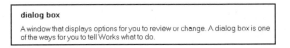

6 Click outside of the pop-up window to close the glossary definition.

Tip Many dialog boxes contain a Help command button that opens a Help window with specific information about the options in that dialog box. You can also get help at any time by pressing F1.

Search the Help topics index

1 In the button bar near the top of the Help screen, click the Search button.

The Search dialog box appears.

2 In the text box, type **starting w**

The Help topic "starting Works" in the top list box is now highlighted. The list box automatically scrolls to the topic that most closely matches what you type, as shown in the following illustration.

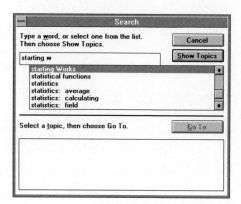

3 Click the Show Topics button.

One or more related topics appear in the bottom list box.

Tip   You can double-click a topic in the top list box to show the related topics in the bottom list box.

---

4 Click the Go To button.

A Help screen appears with information about the "Startup dialog box" topic.

Tip   You can double-click a topic in the bottom list box to display the Help screen for that topic.

View previous Help topics with the Back and History buttons

1 Click the Contents button in the Help window button bar.

2 Click the Back button in the Help window button bar.

The previous Help screen, "Startup dialog box," appears.

3 Click the History button.

The Windows Help History window appears.

The Windows Help History window lists all of the topics you have viewed during the current Help session. The most recently viewed topics are at the top of the list. Notice that the topics you have viewed more than once are repeated in the list.

4 In the Windows Help History window, double-click "Creating a document."

The Help screen for the previously viewed topic, "Creating a document," appears.

View the Glossary list

1 Click the Contents button in the Help window button bar.

2 Under Reference Information, click the topic "Glossary."

The Glossary list appears.

3 Click the H button near the top of the Help window.

Glossary terms that begin with the letter H appear.

4 Click the term "highlight."

A pop-up window appears with the glossary definition of the term "highlight."

5 Click outside of the pop-up window to close the glossary definition.

Note   A Glossary button appears in the Help window button bar when you choose How To Use Help from the Help menu. You can click the Glossary button to access the Windows Help glossary list.

Exit Help

▶ From the Help window File menu, choose Exit.

Control-menu box

Tip   You can also double-click the Control-menu box in the Help window to exit Help.

Quitting Microsoft Works

To quit Works and return to the Program Manager, simply perform the following step.

Quit Microsoft Works

▶ From the File menu, choose Exit Works.

If the Save dialog box appears, click the No button.

Quitting Microsoft Windows

If you would like to quit Windows, execute the following steps.

Quit Windows

1   From the File menu, choose Exit Windows.

A box appears with the message "This will end your Windows session."

2   Press ENTER.

1 Using the Word Processor

Getting Started with the Word Processor

The Works Word Processor is a tool you can use to create any type of text document. You can create letters to business associates, memos to fellow employees, reports for business presentations, and so on. You can dress up your documents by integrating text, numbers, graphics, charts, tables, and objects created with other Works tools.

In this lesson, you'll learn the basics of creating, editing, and printing Word Processor documents. Your company, West Coast Sales, is conducting a special video promotion. The previous department manager created a flyer advertising the savings available on all video titles during the company's annual spring sale. You'll need to make some changes to the flyer to update the information for the current sale.

If your screen does not match the illustrations in this lesson, see the Appendix, "Matching the Exercises."

You will learn how to:

- Start the Word Processor and open a document.
- Type in the Word Processor.
- Save a document.
- Insert blank lines and paragraphs.
- Replace and delete text.
- Copy and move text.
- Preview and print a document.

Estimated lesson time: 20 minutes

Start the lesson

1   If Windows isn't running, start it by typing **win** at the MS-DOS prompt.

2   If Works isn't running, start it by double-clicking the Microsoft Works for Windows icon in the Program Manager window and then double-clicking the Microsoft Works icon in the Microsoft Works for Windows program group window.

Microsoft Works for Windows

Microsoft Works

Note   If you are new to using a mouse, read "If You Are New to Using a Mouse" in the "Getting Ready" section of this book before you start this lesson.

Creating a Word Processor Document

You create a Word Processor document by typing information using the keyboard as you would use a typewriter. However, unlike when you use a typewriter, your work appears on the computer screen rather than on a sheet of paper, so you can view your work before you print it. After you create a document, you can edit your work and save the document for later retrieval.

In the next exercises, you'll create and save a Word Processor document.

Start the Word Processor

Word Processor

1   In the Startup dialog box, click the Word Processor button.

The Word Processor starts and a new document window opens.

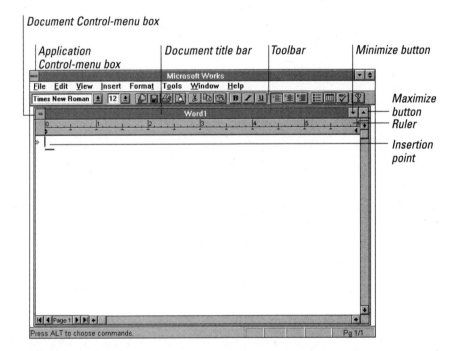

If you want to start a new document, you can just start typing. Since you're going to update an existing document, you will open that document and make changes to it.

Note   When you start the Word Processor from the Startup dialog box, Works always opens a new document window. You can open additional new document windows by choosing the Create New File command from the File menu.

Maximize

2 In the document title bar, click the Maximize button.

The document window now appears *maximized* so that it fills the entire screen. Maximizing enables you to view as much of a document as possible at one time.

Open a document

You can click the Open An Existing Document button in the Startup dialog box to open a document without first starting the Word Processor.

When you installed the practice files in the "Getting Ready" section, the files were copied to your hard disk and stored in the C:\MSWORKS\WORKSSBS directory. To locate and access the files, you must make the directory in which they are stored the current directory.

1 From the File menu, choose Open Existing File.

The Open dialog box appears.

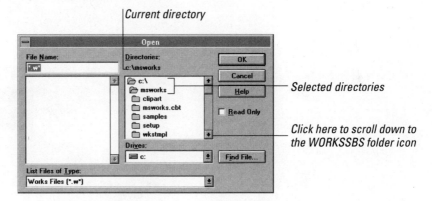

To make C:\MSWORKS\WORKSSBS the current directory, you must select each of the component directories (C:\, MSWORKS, and WORKSSBS). To select a directory, you double-click the corresponding folder icon. When a directory is selected, its icon appears as an open folder.

Note If the C:\ and MSWORKS folder icons are already open, C:\MSWORKS is the current directory. If this is the case, you can skip to step 3.

---

2 In the Directories list box, double-click the C:\ folder icon and then double-click the MSWORKS folder icon to make C:\MSWORKS the current directory.

3 Scroll down in the Directories list box and then double-click the WORKSSBS folder icon to open the directory in which the practice files are stored.

Now that you have selected the WORKSSBS directory, a list of available files appears in the File Name list box, as shown in the following illustration.

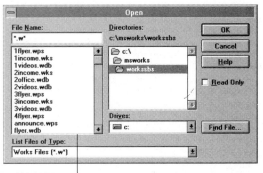

A list of available files appears here

4 In the File Name list box, double-click 1FLYER.WPS.

The file opens.

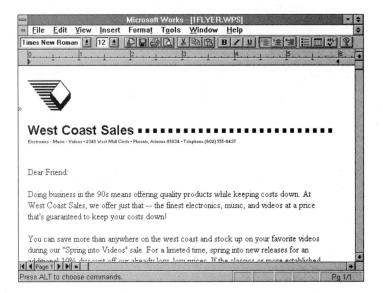

Type in the Word Processor

Now that you have opened your document, you can begin to update the flyer for the
current sale.

1 Click to the right of the double hyphens (--) in the first paragraph.

The mouse pointer appears as an *insertion point*, which is a blinking vertical line
that marks where characters will appear on the screen as you type.

2 Press SPACEBAR and then type **a way to provide quality entertainment to you with**

As you type, you don't have to be concerned about how much text will fit on each line because Works automatically figures out what can fit between the document margins and shifts the text appropriately. This feature is called *word wrap*.

Tip If you make a mistake while typing, you can press BACKSPACE to delete characters to the left of the insertion point. After you delete your mistake, you can continue typing.

Save a document

As you create or change a document, your work is held in the computer's temporary memory. To ensure that you don't lose data, you should make sure you save your document periodically.

1 From the File menu, choose Save As.

The Save As dialog box appears with the current filename highlighted in the File Name text box.

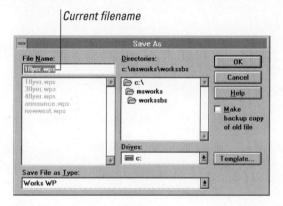

Current filename

2 Type **flyer1** in the File Name text box and then press ENTER.

The document has now been saved as FLYER1.WPS, as indicated in the document title bar. The original file, 1FLYER.WPS, is left in its original form.

Editing a Word Processor Document

When you use the Word Processor to create a document, you have the freedom to make any changes you want quickly and easily. For example, you can add a few words or many paragraphs, replace existing text with new text, delete text that you no longer need, or duplicate and rearrange information.

Making changes to document text is called *editing*. Fortunately, with the Word Processor you can see all of your editing on the screen before you print so that you do not waste time and paper. In the next exercises, you'll add a blank line and a paragraph and replace, copy, delete, and rearrange text in your flyer.

Insert a blank line and a paragraph

1 Click after the exclamation point (!) at the end of the second paragraph.

2 Press ENTER to begin a new paragraph.

3 Press ENTER again to insert a blank line above the new paragraph.

4 Type **Check out the savings on these great videos:**

Replace text

1 In the second paragraph, double-click the word "videos" near the middle of the first sentence.

Double-clicking a word highlights the word. You highlight text when you want to make changes to a word or a larger block of text. Highlighted text appears in white against a shaded background, as shown in the following illustration.

Double-click a word to highlight it

2 Type **movies** to replace the highlighted word and then press SPACEBAR.

Delete text

1 In the first paragraph, click to the left of the word "with" near the middle of the second sentence.

2 Hold down the mouse button, drag to the right of the word "videos" in the same sentence, and then release the mouse button.

Dragging across a block of text highlights the text, as shown in the next illustration.

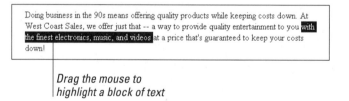

Drag the mouse to highlight a block of text

3 Press DELETE to delete the highlighted text.

Undo a change

If you undo a change and then decide that you want to keep the change after all, you can reverse the undo operation by choosing Redo Editing from the Edit menu.

You can always correct typing errors by pressing BACKSPACE and typing new information. But what if you accidentally delete an entire paragraph? You don't need to retype all of the deleted text. You can reverse the deletion by choosing Undo Editing from the Edit menu.

▶ From the Edit menu, choose Undo Editing.

The block of text you previously deleted is restored to the document. You can use the Undo feature to reverse most typing, editing, and formatting changes; however, you cannot undo an operation such as saving a document.

Note You can undo only the *last* change you made. If you cannot undo a change, the Undo command will appear in dimmed text as Cannot Undo.

Copy text

You can avoid repetitive typing by copying text that already appears in a document.

1 Scroll to the paragraph that begins "While you're checking out our movie savings...."

2 Highlight the words "at West Coast Sales" at the end of the paragraph.

Copy

3 Click the Copy button on the toolbar.

The highlighted text is copied and stored in the Clipboard, which is a temporary storage area in the computer's memory.

4 Click to the left of the period at the end of the last paragraph.

5 Press SPACEBAR.

Paste

6 Click the Paste button on the toolbar.

Works pastes the text from the Clipboard into the document at the insertion point. Your document should now look like the following illustration.

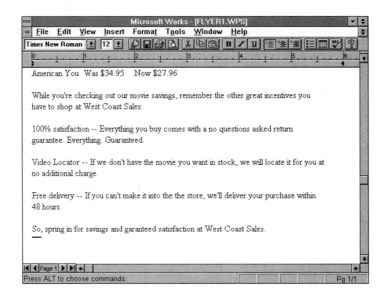

Move text

Instead of deleting text and retyping it in another location, you can simply move the text.

1 Click the blank line above the paragraph that begins "100% satisfaction...."

2 Drag the pointer from the blank line to the end of the following paragraph.

Works highlights the blank line and the paragraph beneath it.

Cut

3 Click the Cut button on the toolbar.

The highlighted text is cut from the document and stored in the Clipboard.

4 Click the blank line below the paragraph that begins "Free delivery...."

Paste

5 Click the Paste button on the toolbar.

Works pastes the text from the Clipboard into the new location. Your screen should look like the following.

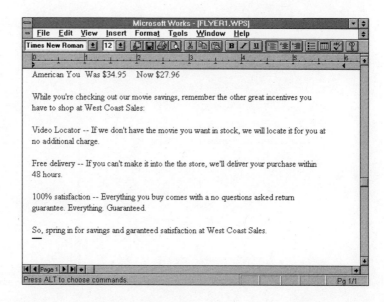

Save

6 Click the Save button on the toolbar to save your changes.

The document is saved with the current name—FLYER1.WPS. The current name appears in the document title bar.

Printing a Word Processor Document

When you are satisfied with the content and appearance of a document, you can print it. Before you print, you can preview your document to see how it will look when printed. Previewing allows you to review the overall layout of a document and spot any areas requiring last minute changes. In the next exercises, you'll preview and print your flyer.

Preview a document before printing

Print Preview

1 Click the Print Preview button on the toolbar.

Your document now appears in the Print Preview window, as shown in the following illustration.

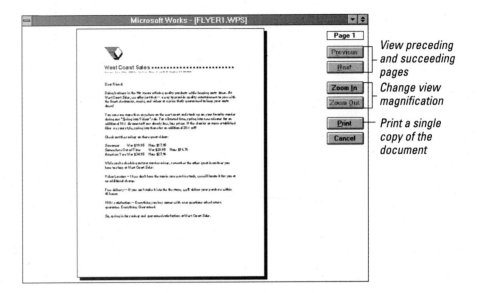

View preceding *and succeeding pages*

Change view *magnification*

Print a single *copy of the document*

If you're having trouble seeing the text in the Print Preview window, you can magnify the view.

You can click a specific area of a document to magnify the view of that area.

2   Click the Zoom In button twice to magnify the view.

3   Click the Zoom Out button twice to shrink the view back to normal magnification.

Note   In a multiple page document, you can click the Previous and Next buttons to preview other pages.

4   When you're done previewing the flyer, click the Cancel button to close the Print Preview window.

Print a document

1   From the File menu, choose Print.

The Print dialog box appears.

Specify the number of copies to print

Print the entire document

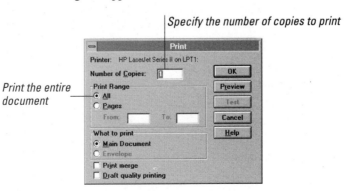

You can set the print options described in the following table.

To	Do this
Print multiple copies	Type the number of copies you want in the Number Of Copies text box.
Print the entire document	Select All under Print Range.
Print specific pages	Select Pages under Print Range and type the numbers of the first and last pages you want to print in the From and To text boxes.
Print a quick copy of the document with minimal formatting	Turn on the Draft Quality Printing check box.

2 Type **2** in the Number Of Copies text box.

3 Click the OK button to print both copies of the document.

The Printing dialog box appears.

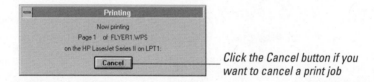

Click the Cancel button if you
want to cancel a print job

The Printing dialog box shows the status of your print job and lists the printer that it is printing on. You can cancel the print job by clicking the Cancel button in the dialog box.

Print

Tip   As a shortcut, you can click the Print button on the toolbar to print a document using the current Print dialog box settings.

One Step Further

Before you move on to the next lesson, you might want to try another editing technique and make one more change to your flyer. Instead of using the Cut and Paste buttons on the toolbar to move text, you can use another method called *drag-and-drop*, which simply entails highlighting text and dragging it with the mouse.

Move text using drag-and-drop

1 Highlight the paragraph that begins "100% satisfaction..." and the blank line beneath it.

2 Position the pointer on the highlighted text.

The pointer changes to the DRAG pointer.

DRAG

MOUE

3   Drag the pointer to the beginning of the paragraph that begins "Video Locator..." and then release the mouse button.

The highlighted text moves to the new location. As you drag the highlighted text, the DRAG pointer changes to the MOVE pointer.

COPY

Note   You can use drag-and-drop to copy text by holding down CTRL as you drag the highlighted text. The pointer changes to the COPY pointer.

Save

4   Click the Save button on the toolbar to save your work.

If You Want to Continue to the Next Lesson

1   Double-click the Document Control-menu box in the menu bar to close FLYER1.WPS.

Document Control-menu box

2   Double-click the Document Control-menu box in the menu bar to close the blank document window.

Application Control-menu box

If You Want to Quit Works for Now

▶   Double-click the Application Control-menu box in the Microsoft Works title bar.

Lesson Summary

To	Do this	Button
Start the Word Processor	Click the Word Processor button in the Startup dialog box.	
Open an existing document	From the File menu, choose Open Existing File, and then double-click the name of the file you want to open in the File Name list box.	
Save an existing document	Click the Save button on the toolbar.	
Save a new document or save a document with a different name.	From the File menu, choose Save As, type a name for the document, and then press ENTER.	
Insert a new paragraph or a blank line	Click where you want the new paragraph or line, and then press ENTER.	
Replace text	Highlight existing text and then type the replacement text.	
Delete text	Highlight the text and then press DELETE.	

To	Do this	Button
Undo a change	From the Edit menu, choose Undo.	
Move text	Highlight the text you want to move, click the Cut button on the toolbar, position the insertion point where you want to move the text, and then click the Paste button on the toolbar.	
Copy text	Highlight the text you want to copy, click the Copy button on the toolbar, position the pointer where you want to copy the text, and then click the Paste button on the toolbar.	
Preview a document	Click the Print Preview button on the toolbar.	
Print a document	From the File menu, choose Print, change print options, and then click the OK button. *or* Click the Print button on the toolbar.	
Move text using drag-and-drop	Highlight the text and then drag the highlighted text to a new location.	
Copy text using drag-and-drop	Highlight the text, hold down CTRL, and then drag the highlighted text to a new location.	

For more information on	See in the *Microsoft Works User's Guide*
Opening a document	Chapter 1, "Naming, saving, duplicating, and reopening a document"
Saving a document	Chapter 3, "Naming and saving a document"
Highlighting text	Chapter 3, "Highlighting to make changes"
Inserting and replacing text	Chapter 3, "Adding text, paragraphs, and lines"
Deleting text	Chapter 3, "Deleting text, charts, drawings, tables, and other objects"
Moving and copying text	Chapter 3, "Copying and moving text, charts, objects, formats, and styles"
Printing a document	Chapter 11, "Printing with Works"

For online information about	From the Help menu, choose Contents and then
Opening a document	Choose "Works for Windows Basic Skills," choose "Working with documents," and select the topic "Opening a document."
Saving a document	Choose "Works for Windows Basic Skills," choose "Working with documents," and select the topic "Saving a document."
Highlighting text	Choose "Works for Windows Basic Skills," choose "Working with documents," and select the topic "Highlighting to make changes."
Inserting and replacing text	Choose "Word Processor," choose "Changing Word Processor information," and select the topic "Adding and replacing text."
Deleting text	Choose "Word Processor," choose "Changing Word Processor information," and select the topic "Deleting information."
Moving and copying text	Choose "Word Processor," choose "Changing Word Processor information," and select the topic "Copying and moving information using the mouse."
Printing a document	Choose "Word Processor," choose "Printing your Word Processor document," and select the topic "Printing Word Processor information."

Preview of the Next Lesson

In this lesson, you opened, edited, and printed your video promotion flyer. In the next lesson, you'll use several formatting features to improve the appearance of your flyer. You'll change the margins, page orientation, line and paragraph spacing, paragraph alignment and indents, tab settings, and fonts. You'll also find and replace text, check spelling, and use the online Thesaurus.

Modifying Word Processor Documents

So far, your video promotion flyer is well organized and it tells your customers what you want them to know. However, you must admit that, overall, it could look better—perhaps a bit flashier. Also, some of the information is more important than other information, so you might want to emphasize certain points and downplay others. You can use Works's formatting features to accomplish these tasks.

Formatting is the process of changing a document to improve its appearance. You can use features like bold or a larger text size to make words or key phrases jump out at the reader, tabs to line up the entries in a table, and indents to make certain paragraphs stand out from the rest.

In this lesson, you'll learn how to use the formatting features of the Word Processor to improve the appearance of your documents. You'll also learn how to use other features to improve your documents. You'll find and replace text in a document, use the Spelling Checker to find and correct misspelled words, and use the Thesaurus to look up a synonym.

If your screen does not match the illustrations in this lesson, see the Appendix, "Matching the Exercises."

You will learn how to:

- Change margins and the page orientation.
- Change line and paragraph spacing.
- Set paragraph alignment and indents.
- Insert and change tabs.
- Work with fonts.
- Find and replace text.
- Use the Spelling Checker and Thesaurus.

Estimated lesson time: 30 minutes

Start the lesson

1 In the Startup dialog box, click the Open An Existing Document button.
2 Make sure C:\MSWORKS\WORKSSBS is the current directory.
3 In the File Name list box, double-click 3FLYER.WPS.

 3FLYER.WPS is identical to the document you completed in Lesson 1.

4 If the 3FLYER.WPS document doesn't completely fill the Word Processor window, click the Maximize button in the document title bar.

Maximize

Changing the Page Setup

The page setup controls the layout of the pages in a document. You can use the Page Setup command to change settings like margins and orientation. In the following exercises, you'll change the margins and the page orientation of your flyer.

Change margins

Currently, the left and right margins of the document have a large amount of blank space. You can reduce the amount of blank space by changing the margins.

1   From the File menu, choose Page Setup.

The Page Setup dialog box appears with margin options.

2   Double-click the Left Margin text box and then type **.75**

3   Press TAB to move to the Right Margin text box, type **.75**, and then press TAB.

The left and right margin settings are now .75 inches. The Sample section of the dialog box illustrates the new margin settings.

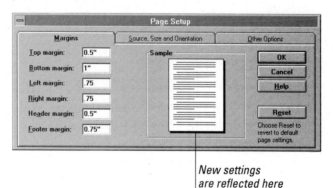

New settings
are reflected here

Note   You can click the Reset button in the Page Setup dialog box to change the margins back to the original settings.

---

4   Press ENTER.

The margins change to reflect the new settings.

Change the page orientation

1   From the File menu, choose Page Setup.

2   Click the Source, Size And Orientation tab.

The current orientation is portrait (vertical), as shown in the Sample section of the dialog box.

3 Under Orientation, select Landscape.

The orientation is now set to landscape (horizontal). The Sample section illustrates the new orientation.

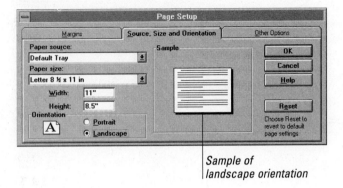

Sample of
landscape orientation

4 Click the OK button.

The page orientation has changed to landscape. To view your document in landscape mode, you must preview the document.

Print Preview

5 Click the Print Preview button on the toolbar.

With landscape orientation, your flyer looks less like a standard letter.

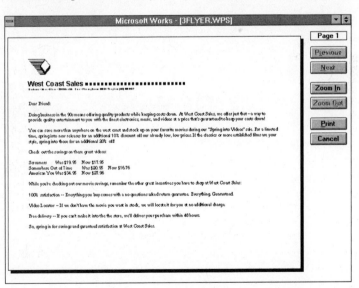

6 Click the Cancel button to close the Print Preview window.

Changing Spacing

You can use spacing features to control the amount of space between the lines and paragraphs in your documents. *Line spacing* determines the amount of space between each line in a paragraph. *Paragraph spacing* determines the amount of space above and below a paragraph. Changing line and paragraph spacing creates distinctions between blocks of text, making them easier to read. Although you can press ENTER to insert blank lines in a document, the spacing features allow you to add spaces of varying size. In the next exercises, you'll change line and paragraph spacing to make your flyer easier to read.

Change line spacing

1 Scroll down and click anywhere in the table of video titles and prices.

The table is a single paragraph. You don't need to highlight a paragraph to change its formats; you need only to click somewhere within the paragraph.

2 From the Format menu, choose Paragraph.

The Paragraph dialog box appears.

3 Click the Breaks And Spacing tab.

4 In the Between Lines text box, type **1.4**

The Paragraph dialog box should look like the following.

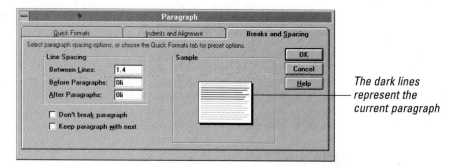

The dark lines represent the current paragraph

5 Press ENTER.

The new line spacing is applied to the current paragraph, as shown in the following illustration.

Screamers	Was $19.95	Now $17.95
Somewhere Out of Time	Was $20.95	Now $16.76
American You	Was $34.95	Now $27.96

Change paragraph spacing

1   Click the blank line below the paragraph that begins "100% satisfaction...."

Since this paragraph and the two that follow it are related, they might look better with less space between them.

2   Press DELETE to delete the blank line.

3   Delete the blank line below the paragraph that begins "Video Locator...."

4   Highlight the three paragraphs ("100% satisfaction...," "Video Locator...," and "Free delivery..."), as shown in the following illustration.

5   From the Format menu, choose Paragraph.

You use the Before Paragraphs and After Paragraphs options to add extra space before and after paragraphs. You can specify paragraph spacing as a whole number or a decimal.

6   Click in the After Paragraphs text box.

7   Type **.45** and then press ENTER.

Works adds .45 lines of space after each highlighted paragraph.

Note   It's a good practice to add space after paragraphs rather than before them so the extra spacing does not appear at the top of a subsequent page.

---

8   Click the blank line below the paragraphs to deselect the paragraphs.

Setting Alignment

Alignment determines how paragraphs are positioned between the left and right document margins. In a new document, all paragraphs are left-aligned. To call attention to certain paragraphs, you can change the paragraph alignment to center-aligned, right-aligned, or justified.

To apply the same alignment to two or more paragraphs at the same time, you must highlight the paragraphs first. If you want to change the alignment of only a single paragraph, just click anywhere in the paragraph to start. In the next exercises, you'll set the alignment for multiple paragraphs and a single paragraph.

Set the alignment for multiple paragraphs

1   Starting with the paragraph that begins "Doing business in the 90s...," highlight all paragraphs down to the end of the document.

2 From the Format menu, choose Paragraph.

3 Click the Indents And Alignment tab.

Indent and alignment options appear in the Paragraph dialog box.

4 Under Alignment, select Justified.

The Sample section of the dialog box now shows justified alignment.

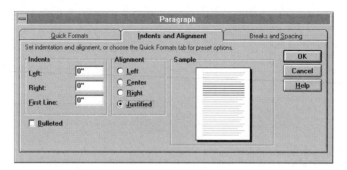

5 Click the OK button.

With justified alignment, paragraphs align evenly between the left and right margins.

Set the alignment for a single paragraph

1 Click in the paragraph that begins "Check out the savings...."

Center Align

2 Click the Center Align button on the toolbar.

The paragraph is now centered between the left and right margins.

3 Click in the table of video titles and prices.

Left Align

4 Click the Left Align button on the toolbar.

The alignment of the table changes from justified to left-aligned.

The table is now left-aligned

Check out the savings on these great videos:

Screamers   Was $19.95   Now $17.95
Somewhere Out of Time   Was $20.95   Now $16.76
American You Was $34.95   Now $27.96

While you're checking out our movie savings, remember the other great incentives you have to shop

5 From the File menu, choose Save As.

6 Type **flyer3** in the File Name text box and then press ENTER.

Setting Indents and Adding Bullets

Indents control the amount of space between a paragraph and the left and right margins. You use indents to make certain paragraphs stand out from others. Bullets also set certain items apart from others. In the next exercises, you'll indent the paragraph of video titles and prices and add bullets to other paragraphs.

Indent a paragraph

1 Be sure the insertion point is in the paragraph of video titles and prices.

The ruler contains indent markers that you can drag to indent the current paragraph.

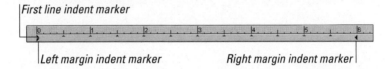

First line indent marker

Left margin indent marker   Right margin indent marker

When you drag the left margin indent marker, the first line indent marker will move with it. If you want to set a first line indent, you can drag the first line indent marker independently.

2 Drag the left margin indent marker to the 2 inch mark on the ruler.

The current paragraph is indented 2 inches from the left margin, as shown in the next illustration.

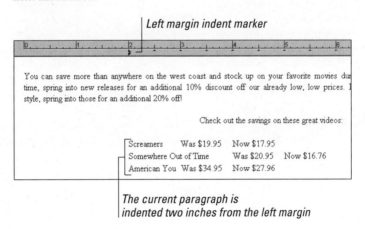

Left margin indent marker

You can save more than anywhere on the west coast and stock up on your favorite movies dur time, spring into new releases for an additional 10% discount off our already low, low prices. I style, spring into those for an additional 20% off!

Check out the savings on these great videos:

Screamers   Was $19.95   Now $17.95
Somewhere Out of Time   Was $20.95   Now $16.76
American You Was $34.95   Now $27.96

The current paragraph is indented two inches from the left margin

Add bullets

1 Highlight the paragraph that begins "100% satisfaction..." and the two paragraphs beneath it.

Bullets

2 Click the Bullets button on the toolbar.

Works inserts bullets in front of the highlighted paragraphs.

3 Scroll to the left to see the bullets.

Tip   To turn off bullets, highlight the bulleted text, choose Paragraph from the Format menu, click the Indents And Alignment tab, and then turn off the Bulleted check box.

Working with Tabs

Like you use indents, you can use tabs to make certain paragraphs stand out in a document. You can use tabs to indent the first line of a paragraph, and you usually use tabs to line up columns of information in a table. When you press TAB, the insertion point moves from its current location to the next tab stop. Existing text and text that you type aligns at the tab stop, based on the style of the tab. You can choose from the tab styles shown in the following illustration.

Left	**Center**	**Right**	**Decimal**
horses	horses	horses	12.34
dogs	dogs	dogs	3,216.22
cats	cats	cats	.46
parakeets	parakeets	parakeets	1,200,456,900.01

In a new document, tabs for all paragraphs are left-aligned and preset at every .5 inches. The preset tabs work well for paragraph indents, but they aren't always appropriate for a table of information. Fortunately, you can easily insert and adjust tabs and change tab styles. In the next exercises, you'll insert and adjust tabs so that the information in the table of video titles and prices is aligned properly in columns and stands out from the rest of the paragraphs. You'll also add more information to the table.

Insert tabs

1   Click in the table of video titles and prices.

The ruler contains tab markers that show you the tab settings for the current paragraph. The markers you currently see are default tab markers.

Default tab marker

2   Click below the 4.5 inch mark on the ruler.

A custom tab marker (**t**) is inserted on the ruler and the second column of information in the table aligns at the position of the tab marker.

3   Click below the 6 inch mark on the ruler.

Another custom tab marker is inserted on the ruler and the third column of information in the table aligns at the position of the tab marker.

Adjust tabs

1 If necessary, click the scroll arrow on the right side of the horizontal scroll bar a few times to bring the entire table into view, as it is in the next illustration.

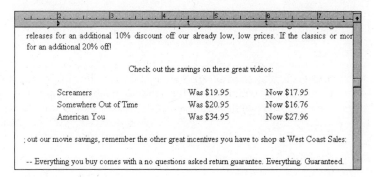

The third column of information could be moved a bit more to the right.

2 Drag the tab marker at the 6 inch mark to the 6.5 inch mark on the ruler.

Adjusting the tab stop makes the spacing between the columns more uniform, as shown in the following illustration.

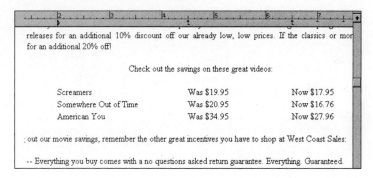

Add leader characters

Leaders are characters, such as dots, that appear between tab stops. Leaders can make a table easier to read.

1 From the Format menu, choose Tabs.

The Tabs dialog box appears, as shown in the following illustration.

Alignment
options

Leader
options

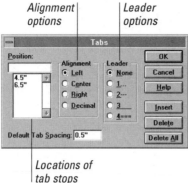

Locations of
tab stops

2 In the Position list box, select 4.5".

3 Under Leader, select **1**... and then click the Insert button to assign the first leader style to the tab at the 4.5 inch mark.

4 In the Position list box, select 6.5".

5 Under Leader, select **1**... and then click the OK button to assign the first leader style to the tab at the 6.5 inch mark and close the Tabs dialog box.

Works inserts leaders between the tabs in the table. Your table should now match the table shown in the following illustration.

Check out the savings on these great videos:

Screamers...Was $19.95...........................Now $17.95
Somewhere Out of Time.....................Was $20.95...........................Now $16.76
American You.......................................Was $34.95...........................Now $27.96

Add text to a table

1 Click at the end of the third line in the table of video titles and prices.

2 Press SHIFT+ENTER to start a new line in the same paragraph.

Note   Pressing ENTER creates a new paragraph; pressing SHIFT+ENTER starts a new line without creating a new paragraph. Keeping all the lines of a table together in a single paragraph allows you to format the entire table as one paragraph.

3 Type **Falling from Love** and then press TAB.

Works inserts leaders and the insertion point moves to the next tab stop.

4 Type **Was $17.99**, press TAB, and then type **Now $14.39**

Your table should now look like the following illustration.

Check out the savings on these great videos:

Screamers.................................Was $19.95.........................Now $17.95
Somewhere Out of Time..................Was $20.95.........................Now $16.76
American You.............................Was $34.95.........................Now $27.96
Falling from Love........................Was $17.99.........................Now $14.39

Working with Fonts

A *font* is a set of characters with a specific design and a similar appearance. Each font has its own name, such as Arial or Times New Roman, which you use to identify and select the font. Each font usually has a variety of sizes and styles. The size of a font is measured in *points*, with one point equal to approximately 1/72 inch. You generally use a 10-point or 12-point font for basic text, and larger fonts for headlines and titles. You can change the style of a font by applying bold, italic, or underline styles. The following illustration shows examples of different fonts, point sizes, and styles.

Arial 10-point Italic

Times New Roman 12-point Normal

Roman 12-point Underline

Modern 14-point Normal

Arial 18-point Bold

Use different fonts, sizes, and styles in a document when you want to improve the appearance and readability of text, emphasize key words and ideas, or fit more text on a printed page. In the next exercises, you'll change the font, size, and style of text to enhance your flyer.

Change the font

1 Hold down CTRL and click in the left margin.

   Works highlights all of the text in the document.

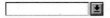

Font Name list box

2 Click the arrow to the right of the Font Name list box on the toolbar.

   The font list shows you the names of the available fonts.

3 Select Arial to change the font of the highlighted text.

Change the font size

1   Starting with the blank line below the paragraph near the top of the document that begins "Electronics - Music - Videos," highlight all paragraphs down to the end of the document.

Font Size list box

2   Click the arrow to the right of the Font Size list box on the toolbar.

3   Select 10 to change the point size of the highlighted text.

4   Highlight the paragraph that begins "Electronics - Music - Videos...."

5   Click the arrow to the right of the Font size list box on the toolbar and then select 8.

Add bold, italic, and underline

1   Highlight the paragraph that begins "Check out the savings...."

Bold

2   Click the Bold button on the toolbar to bold the highlighted text.

3   In the first paragraph, highlight the text "at a price that's guaranteed to keep your costs down!"

Italic

4   Click the Italic button on the toolbar to italicize the highlighted text.

5   At the end of the first bulleted paragraph, highlight the text "Everything. Guaranteed."

Underline

6   Click the Underline button on the toolbar to underline the highlighted text.

7   Click above the underlined text.

Your screen should now look like the following.

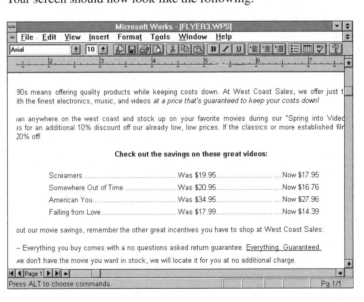
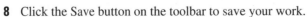

8   Click the Save button on the toolbar to save your work.

Save

Finding and Replacing Text

If you need to replace text in a document, you don't have to manually scroll through the document, search for the text, and change it. Instead, you can use the find and replace features to quickly search for a word or phrase and automatically replace it with a different word or phrase. You can replace text throughout an entire document or you can limit your search to a highlighted block. In the next exercise, you'll replace the word "movie," everywhere it appears in your flyer, with the word "video."

Replace text

To position the cursor at the end of a document, press CTRL+END.

1 Press CTRL+HOME to position the insertion point at the top of the document.

2 From the Edit menu, choose Replace.

The Replace dialog box appears.

Note   If you want to only find a word or phrase, not replace it with other text, choose Find from the Edit menu.

---

3 Type **movie** in the Find What text box.

This is the text you want to find.

4 Press TAB to move to the Replace With text box, and then type **video**

This is the replacement text. The Replace dialog box should now appear as follows.

5 Click the Find Next button.

Works highlights the first occurrence of the word "movie."

6 Click the Replace button.

Works replaces the first occurrence of "movie" with "video" and highlights the next occurrence.

7 Click the Replace All button.

Works makes the remaining replacements without stopping at each occurrence.

8 Click the Close button.

Using the Spelling Checker and Thesaurus

Works has two accessories you can use to improve language usage in your documents. You can use the Spelling Checker, a 113,664-word electronic dictionary, to find and correct misspelled words. If you find yourself using the same word repeatedly, you can use the 200,000-word Thesaurus to look up a *synonym*, which is a different word with the same or similar meaning. In the next exercises, you'll check your flyer for misspelled words and look up a synonym.

Correct misspelled words

1 If the insertion point is not at the top of the document, press CTRL+HOME.

2 Click the Spelling Checker button on the toolbar.

Works highlights the first misspelled word, "limeted," and opens the Spelling dialog box.

3 Turn on the Always Suggest check box and then click the Suggest button.

A list of alternative words appears in the Suggestions list box.

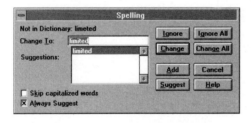

Spelling Checker

To turn on a check box, click the check box so that an X appears in it.

When you turn on the Always Suggest check box, Works will display a list of alternative words for every misspelled word it encounters.

If you want to check the spelling in only a portion of your document, highlight that portion before you start the spelling check.

4 Click the Change button.

Works changes "limeted" to "limited." The next highlighted word, "the," is a repeated word.

5 Click the Change button.

Works deletes the duplicate word and highlights the next misspelled word, "garanteed."

6 Click the Change button.

Works changes "garanteed" to "guaranteed" and displays the Spelling Check Finished information box.

7   Click the OK button.

Find a synonym

1   In the paragraph that begins "While you're checking out...," click anywhere in the word "incentives."

This word doesn't convey quite the feeling you want.

2   From the Tools menu, choose Thesaurus.

3   Click the Suggest button.

The Thesaurus dialog box appears with a list of suggested synonyms, as shown in the following illustration.

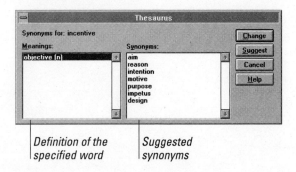

Definition of the specified word   Suggested synonyms

4   In the Synonyms list box, select "reason," and then click the Change button.

Works changes "incentives" to "reason" in the document.

5   Type **s** to make the new word plural.

6   Save your work.

One Step Further

So far, you've learned a number of exciting features you can use to make your documents more attractive. Why not try one more feature, called *paragraph borders*, to make the table of video titles and prices in your flyer really stand apart from the rest of the text. Paragraph borders are lines and boxes you can place around paragraphs to draw attention to important information. You can also use them to underline headings or separate sections in a document.

Add a paragraph border

1   Click in the paragraph that begins "Check out the savings...."

2   From the Format menu, choose Border.

3   Under Border, turn on the Outline check box.

4   Under Line Style, select Bold.

The settings in the Border dialog box should now match the following illustration.

5   Click the OK button.

A bold border appears around the paragraph. The border extends to the left and right margins, but might look better if it is about the same width as the table of video titles. Since the insertion point is currently positioned within the paragraph, you can use the ruler to quickly change the margins of the paragraph border.

6   Drag the left margin indent marker to the 2 inch mark on the ruler.

7   Drag the right margin indent marker to the 7.25 inch mark and then scroll left so that the entire table is in view.

The paragraph border should now look like the border shown in the following illustration.

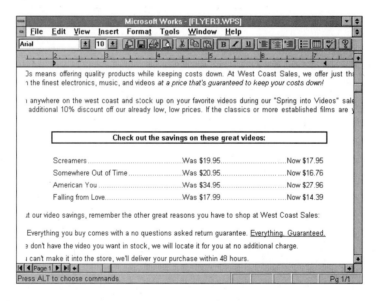

8   Save your work.

If You Want to Continue to the Next Lesson

*Document
Control-menu box*

▶   Double-click the Document Control-menu box in the menu bar to close FLYER3.WPS.

Application
Control-menu box

If You Want to Quit Works for Now

▶ Double-click the Application Control-menu box in the Microsoft Works title bar.

Lesson Summary

To	Do this	Button
Change margins	From the File menu, choose Page Setup, click the Margins tab, type new margin settings, and then press ENTER.	
Change the page orientation	From the File menu, choose Page Setup, click the Source, Size And Orientation tab, select an Orientation option, and then click the OK button.	
Change alignment	Highlight the paragraphs you want to format and then click an alignment button on the toolbar. For justified alignment, choose Paragraph from the Format menu, click the Indents And Alignment tab, select Justified under Alignment, and then click the OK button.	
Indent paragraphs	Highlight the paragraphs you want to format and then drag indent markers on the ruler.	
Insert tabs	Highlight the paragraphs you want to format and then click where you want the tabs to be on the ruler.	
Adjust tabs	Drag the tab markers on the ruler.	
Change the font	Highlight the text you want to format, click the arrow to the right of the Font Name list box on the toolbar, and then select a font.	Times New Roman
Change the font size	Highlight the text you want to format, click the arrow to the right of the Font Size list box on the toolbar, and then select a font size.	12

To	Do this	Button
Change the font style	Highlight the text you want to format and then click the Bold, Italic, or Underline button on the toolbar.	**B** _I_ <u>U</u>
Replace text	From the Tools menu, choose Replace, and then type the search and replacement text. To replace single occurrences, click the Find Next button and then click the Replace button. To replace all occurrences, click the Replace All button.	
Check the spelling of a document	Move to the top of the document and then click the Spelling Checker button on the toolbar.	ABC ✓
Find a synonym	Move the insertion point to a word and then choose Thesaurus from the Tools menu.	
Add a paragraph border	Click in a paragraph, choose Border from the Format menu, select Border and Line Style options, and then click the OK button.	

For more information on	See in the *Microsoft Works User's Guide*
Changing the page setup	Chapter 3, "Changing page and margin settings"
Changing spacing	Chapter 3, "Line spacing" Chapter 3, "Changing spacing around paragraphs and controlling page breaks"
Setting alignment	Chapter 3, "Setting alignment to visually organize paragraphs"
Setting indents and tabs	Chapter 3, "Indenting paragraphs to visually organize a document" Chapter 3, "Creating bulleted lists and other lists with tabs and indents"
Working with fonts	Chapter 3, "Using the toolbar" Chapter 3, "Changing fonts, font sizes, font styles, and colors"
Finding and replacing text	Chapter 3, "Finding and replacing text and special characters"
Using the Spelling Checker and Thesaurus	Chapter 10, "Checking spelling" Chapter 3, "Using the Thesaurus and counting words"
Adding paragraph borders	Chapter 3, "Placing borders around a paragraph"

For online information about	From the Help menu, choose Contents and then
Changing the page setup	Choose "Word Processor," choose "Printing your Word Processor documents," and select the topic "Setting page size, margins, and orientation."
Changing spacing	Choose "Word Processor," choose "Changing the appearance of your Word Processor document," and select the topic "Setting line and paragraph spacing."
Setting alignment	Choose "Word Processor," choose "Changing the appearance of your Word Processor document," and select the topic "Aligning paragraphs."
Setting indents and tabs	Choose "Word Processor," choose "Changing the appearance of your Word Processor document," and select the topic "Indenting paragraphs."
Working with fonts	Choose "Word Processor," choose "Changing the appearance of your Word Processor document," and select the topic "Changing text appearance and size."
Finding and replacing text	Choose "Word Processor," choose "Word Processor basics," and select the topic "Replacing text and special characters."
Using the Spelling Checker and Thesaurus	Choose "Word Processor," choose "Word Processor basics," and select either "Checking spelling and counting" or "Thesaurus."
Adding a paragraph border	Choose "Word Processor," choose "Changing the appearance of your Word Processor document," and select the topic "Borders."

Preview of the Next Lesson

Congratulations! You are now able to create, edit, and format accurate and attractive documents that inform and capture the attention of the reader. If you want to learn how to add a personal touch to your documents and automate some of the tasks you have learned, move on to the next lesson, in which you'll learn how to produce personalized form letters, mailing labels, and envelopes.

Creating Complex Documents

The information you have learned about the Works Word Processor so far is probably sufficient if you plan on writing only simple letters, memos, or flyers. However, if you want to efficiently create more complex documents—such as form letters with personalized information and matching envelopes—you'll need to learn a little bit more about the Word Processor. The process for creating form letters, mailing labels, and envelopes is more elaborate than the process you used to create your video promotion flyer. But don't worry! Works provides features that make the production of such complex documents quick and easy: WorksWizards and the print merge feature.

WorksWizards are automated processes that you can use to perform tasks such as creating form letters, as well as creating custom stationery, designing a database, adding footnotes to a document, and organizing files on your hard drive. Using a WorksWizard is easy. A series of screens appear with questions about the task you want to perform. All you need to do is answer the questions, and the WorksWizard will do the rest.

The *print merge* feature combines information from two documents into a single document in a specified sequence. You can use print merge to automate the production of mailing labels and envelopes. In this lesson, you'll use a WorksWizard to personalize each of your video promotion flyers with the customer's name and address and then use print merge to print matching envelopes or mailing labels.

If your screen does not match the illustrations in this lesson, see the Appendix, "Matching the Exercises."

You will learn how to:

- Produce personalized form letters, mailing labels, and envelopes.

Estimated lesson time: 20 minutes

Start the lesson

▶ Be sure the Startup dialog box is open.

Producing Form Letters

For more information about databases, see the Microsoft Works User's Guide, *Chapter 6, "Guide to the database."*

Form letters are multiple copies of the same document with personalized information, such as names and addresses, inserted in each copy of the document. You produce form letters by inserting information from a Works database file into a Word Processor document. The following steps outline the basic process for producing form letters:

- Create or open the Word Processor document containing the standard text that will appear in every copy of the form letter.

- Select the database file containing the personalized information you want to include in the form letters.

- Insert placeholders in the letter at locations where you want to merge personalized information from the database file.

- Preview and print the form letters.

You can automate this process by using a WorksWizard.

In the next exercises, you'll use a WorksWizard to personalize and print your video promotion flyers with each customer's name, address, and video type preference.

Start the WorksWizard

1 In the Startup dialog box, click the Use A WorksWizard button.

The Startup dialog box now appears with a list of available WorksWizards.

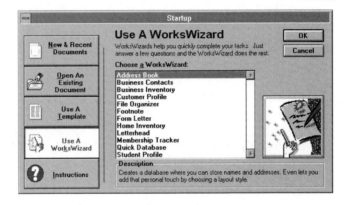

2 In the Choose A WorksWizard list box, double-click Form Letter.

The Form Letter WorksWizard opens, as shown in the next illustration.

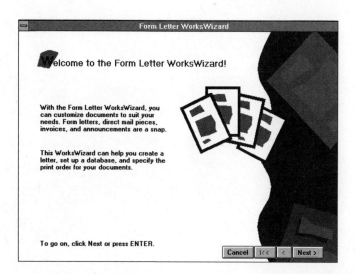

3 Click the Next > button.

As you go through the Form Letter WorksWizard, you will be asked a series of questions about the information that will comprise the form letters. The WorksWizard is currently asking if there is an existing database that contains the personalized information that you want to put into the letters. There is already a database with all of the customer information that you will put into the letters.

4 Select Yes if it isn't already selected, and then click the Next > button.

The WorksWizard now asks if there is an existing letter to use. You'll use a flyer similar to the one created in Lesson 2 as the letter.

5 Select Yes if it isn't already selected, and then click the Next > button.

The WorksWizard now displays a list of available Word Processor files. If the file containing the letter you want to use appears in the list, you can click the Open button to open the file. If your file doesn't appear in the list, you can look for it by clicking the search button, and then open it.

If you didn't have an existing database to use, you would select No in the Form Letter WorksWizard. Selecting this option closes the WorksWizard and gives you a choice of several WorksWizards you can use to create a database.

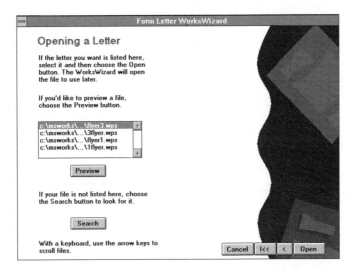

Open the letter

1 Click the Search button, type **4flyer**, and then click the Search button.

A list of all files with the text "4FLYER" in the name now appears in the WorksWizard.

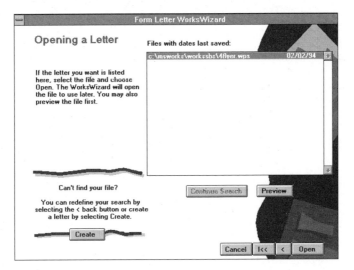

2 Click C:\MSWORKS\WORKSSBS\4FLYER.WPS if it is not already highlighted.

3 Click the Open button to open 4FLYER.WPS.

Now you need to open the database file containing the personalized information that will appear in the form letters.

Open the database

1 Click the Search button, type **flyer**, and then click the Search button.

A list of all files with the text "FLYER.WDB" in the name now appears in the WorksWizard.

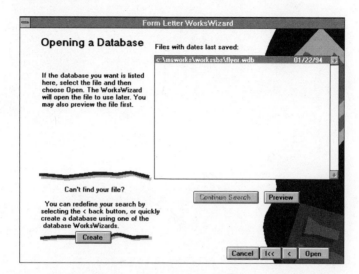

2 Click C:\MSWORKS\WORKSSBS\FLYER.WDB if it isn't already highlighted.

3 Click the Open button to open FLYER.WDB.

The WorksWizard now displays simple instructions for completing the process of creating form letters.

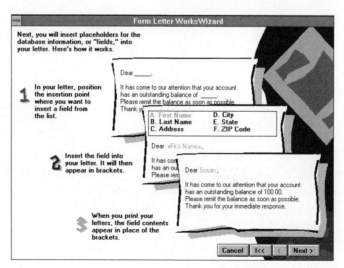

4   Click the Next > button.

The next WorksWizard screen that appears shows brief instructions for inserting database fields into the 4FLYER.WPS document.

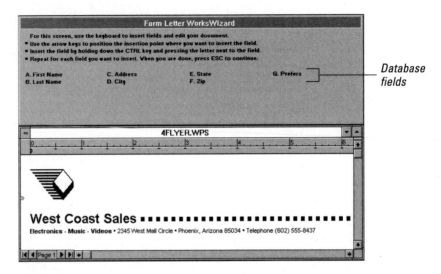

Database fields

The field names that appear in the top portion of the screen match the field names in the FLYER.WDB database. You are now ready to insert database fields into the Word Processor document.

Insert the database fields

Each database field that you insert into the document is represented by a placeholder, which is replaced by the field contents when you print the form letters.

1   Use the arrow keys to position the cursor on the blank line above "Dear Friend:"

2   Hold down CTRL and type **a**

The First Name field placeholder appears in the flyer.

3   Press SPACEBAR and then hold down CTRL and type **b**

4   Press ENTER and then hold down CTRL and type **c**

5   Press ENTER and then hold down CTRL and type **d**

6   Type **,** and then press SPACEBAR.

7   Insert the State field placeholder and then press SPACEBAR.

8   Insert the Zip field placeholder and then press ENTER.

9   Use the arrow keys to position the insertion point to the left of the colon (:) in "Dear Friend:"

10 Press BACKSPACE six times to delete "Friend."

11 Insert the First Name field placeholder.

12   Use the arrow keys to display the second line in the second paragraph, position the insertion point to the right of the word "favorite," and then press SPACEBAR.

13   Insert the Prefers field placeholder.

Your screen should now match the following illustration.

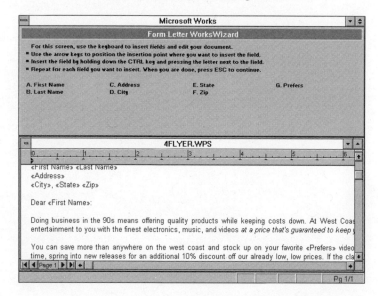

14   Press ESC to indicate that you are done inserting placeholders.

You have now supplied all the information necessary to create your form letters. At this point, the WorksWizard asks if you want to print form letters for all the records in the database or for only some of the records. You will print letters for all of them.

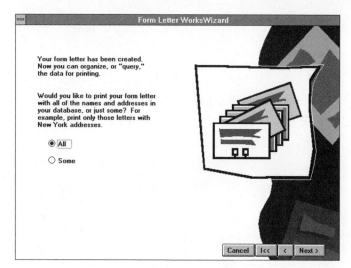

Complete the WorksWizard

1 Click the Next > button.

At this point, you can decide if you want to print the letters in a specified order. You will keep the letters in their current order.

2 Select No Sort, Thanks and then click the Next > button.

The WorksWizard is now completed. The following screen should appear.

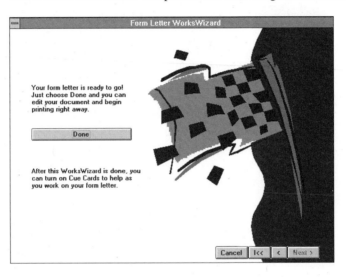

Maximize

3 Click the Done button and then click the maximize button in the 4FLYER.WPS title bar to maximize the document so that it fills the entire window.

4 From the File menu, choose Save As.

5 Type **flyer4** and then press ENTER.

Preview the form letters

Before printing, you can preview the form letters to make sure that all the specified information appears where it should.

Print Preview

1 Click the Print Preview button on the toolbar.

The Choose Database dialog box appears.

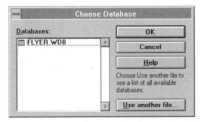

2   In the Databases list box, double-click FLYER.WDB.

The first form letter appears in the Print Preview window.

3   Click the Zoom In button and then click the Next button five times to preview all of the form letters.

All of the form letters contain personalized information at the location of each placeholder.

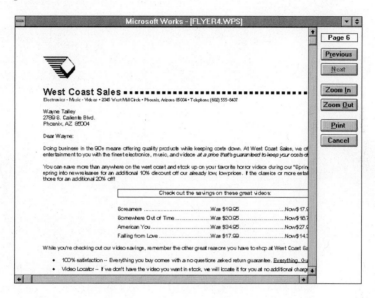

4   Click the Cancel button to close the Print Preview window.

Print the form letters

The only time that data from the database is actually inserted in the form letter is when it is printed. The print merge feature merges the information from each document. Because the Word Processor document contains placeholders, Works knows that it is a print merge file.

1   From the File menu, choose Print.

The Print Merge option is automatically turned on in the Print dialog box.

2   Click the OK button.

The Choose Database dialog box appears.

3   In the Databases list box, double-click FLYER.WDB.

The Printing dialog box appears, as shown in the next illustration.

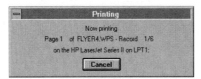

Note   If you don't want to merge and print all of the database records, you must first hide the records that you don't want to print. For information about hiding database records, see Lesson 9, "Getting Started with the Database."

4 When your form letters have finished printing, double-click the Document Control-menu box in the menu bar to close FLYER4.WPS.

Document Control-menu box

5 Double-click the Document Control-menu box in the title bar of FLYER.WDB.

The document closes and the Startup dialog box appears.

Producing Mailing Labels

After you print your form letters, you can create mailing labels with matching names and addresses. Like form letters, you create mailing labels by inserting placeholders from a database file in a Word Processor document. You follow these steps to produce mailing labels:

- Open a Word Processor document to store the mailing label placeholders.
- Select a database file and insert placeholders in the Word Processor document.
- Select a label style and create the labels.
- Preview, test, and print the mailing labels.

Since there is no WorksWizard for creating mailing labels, you must insert the placeholders manually and use the print merge feature to create the labels.

In the next exercises, you'll create and print mailing labels that match the names and addresses on your video promotion form letters.

Word Processor

Open a Word Processor document

▶ In the Startup dialog box, click the Word Processor button, and then maximize the document window.

Select a database

1 From the Tools menu, choose Envelopes And Labels.

The Envelopes And Labels dialog box appears.

2 Click the Mailing Labels tab.

3 Click the Fields>> button.

The Current Database box shows "None," indicating that no database is available.

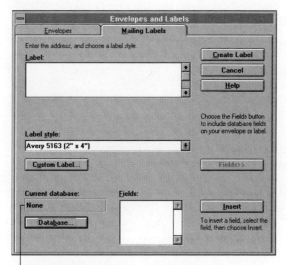

| No database is currently available

4 Click the Database button.

The Choose Database dialog box appears.

5 Double-click FLYER.WDB to select the database.

Insert placeholders

Now that you have selected the FLYER.WDB database, field names from the database appear in the Fields list box of the Envelopes And Labels dialog box. Double-clicking a field name in the Fields list box places a corresponding placeholder in the Label text box. These placeholders will be inserted in the blank Word Processor document when you create the labels.

1 In the Fields list box, double-click First Name.

Works inserts the <<First Name>> placeholder in the Label text box.

2 Press SPACEBAR and then double-click Last Name in the Fields list box.

3 Press ENTER and then double-click the Address field.

4 Press ENTER and then double-click the City field.

5 Type ,

6 Press SPACEBAR and then double-click the State field.

7 Press SPACEBAR and then double-click the Zip field.

The Envelopes And Labels dialog box should now appear as follows.

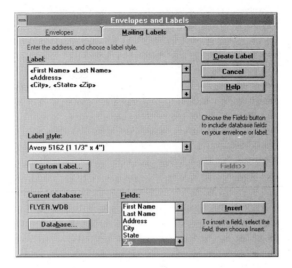

Select a label style and create the labels

Now that you have inserted placeholders, all you need to do is select a label style and create the labels.

1 If the entry in the Label Style list box is not Avery 5162 (1 1/3" x 4"), click the arrow to the right of the Label Style list box, and select Avery 5162 (1 1/3" x 4").

Note You can click the Custom Label button to specify dimensions for nonstandard labels that are not listed under Label Style.

---

2 Click the Create Label button.

Works inserts the placeholders in the Word Processor document.

Save

3 Click the Save button on the toolbar to open the Save As dialog box.

4 Save the document as MAILING.WPS in the C:\MSWORKS\WORKSSBS directory.

Your document should now look like the following illustration.

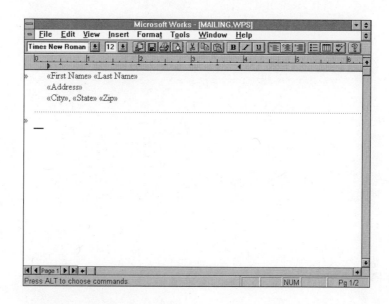

Preview the mailing labels

Print Preview

1   Click the Print Preview button on the toolbar.

2   In the Choose Database dialog box, double-click FLYER.WDB.

The Merge All Records? information box appears, asking you to confirm that you want to merge all of the database records.

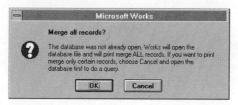

3   Click the OK button to merge all of the database records.

Your Print Preview window should look like the following illustration.

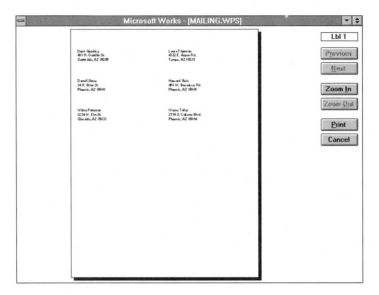

4 Click the Zoom In button to magnify the text so that you can read it.

5 Click the Cancel button to close the Print Preview window.

Print a test row of mailing labels

If you don't have label stock in your printer, you can print the labels on a regular sheet of paper. If you do have label stock, you can print a test row of labels to make sure they align properly in your printer.

1 From the File menu, choose Print.

2 In the Print dialog box, click the Test button.

3 In the Choose Database dialog box, double-click FLYER.WDB.

4 Click the OK button to merge all of the database records.

A test row of labels prints and the Test Label Printing dialog box appears so you can print another test row, adjust the label settings, or print the remaining labels.

5 Click the Cancel button.

Print the mailing labels

Print

1 Click the Print button on the toolbar.

2 In the Choose Database dialog box, double-click FLYER.WDB.

3   Click the OK button to merge and print all of the database records.

4   Close MAILING.WPS.

Producing Envelopes

If your printer is capable of printing directly on envelopes, you can avoid the extra time needed to attach mailing labels to the envelopes. You produce personalized envelopes in much the same way that you produce mailing labels, using the following steps:

- Open a Word Processor document to store the envelope placeholders and a return address.

- Select a database and insert placeholders and the return address text in the Word Processor document.

- Select an envelope size and create the envelopes.

- Preview and print the envelopes.

In the next exercises, you'll produce envelopes that match the personalized information in your video promotion form letters.

Word Processor

Open a Word Processor document

▶   In the Startup dialog box, click the Word Processor button.

Select a database

1   From the Tools menu, choose Envelopes And Labels.

2   Click the Fields>> button.

3   Click the Database button and then double-click FLYER.WDB in the Choose Database dialog box.

Insert placeholders and a return address

1   In the Fields list box, double-click First Name.

Works inserts the <<First Name>> placeholder in the Address text box.

2   Press SPACEBAR and then double-click Last Name in the Fields list box.

3   Press ENTER and then double-click the Address field.

4   Press ENTER and then double-click the City field.

5   Type ,

6   Press SPACEBAR and then double-click the State field.

7   Press SPACEBAR and then double-click the Zip field.

8   Click in the Return Address box and type the return address shown in the following illustration.

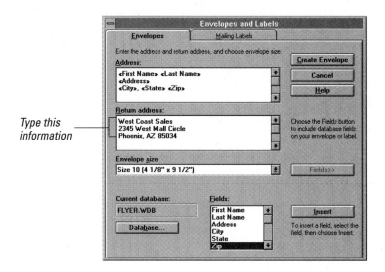

Type this information

Create the envelopes

1   Click the Create Envelope button.

Works inserts the placeholders and return address in the Word Processor document.

2   Save the document as ENVELOPE.WPS in the C:\MSWORKS\WORKSSBS directory.

Your document should now look like the following illustration.

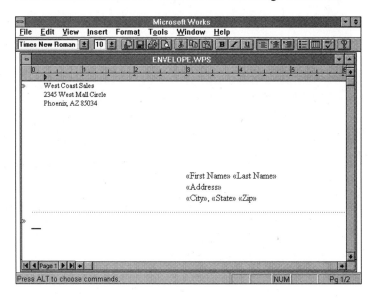

Preview the envelopes

Print Preview

1   Click the Print Preview button on the toolbar.

2   In the Choose Database dialog box, double-click FLYER.WDB.

3   Click the OK button to merge all of the database records.

4   Click the Next button five times to preview the envelopes.

5   Click the Cancel button to close the Print Preview window.

Print the envelopes

Important   If you have an envelope feeder on your printer, you must choose Options from the Tools menu, turn on the Printer's Envelope Feeder Is Installed check box, and then click the OK button before you print. If you don't have an envelope feeder, skip this procedure.

Print

1   Click the Print button on the toolbar.

2   In the Choose Database dialog box, double-click FLYER.WDB.

3   Click the OK button to merge and print all of the database records.

If your printer has an envelope feeder, the envelopes feed and print automatically. If your printer does not have an envelope feeder, you must insert each envelope manually.

4   Close ENVELOPE.WPS.

One Step Further

If you want to address and print a single envelope you can do so without accessing the information in your customer database.

Address and print a single envelope

Word Processor

1   In the Startup dialog box, click the Word Processor button.

2   From the Tools menu, choose Envelopes And Labels.

3   In the Address box, type the following name and address:

Laura Thomson
432 E. Aspen Rd.
Tempe, AZ 85281

4   Click the Create Envelope button to insert the information in the document.

5   Click the Print button on the toolbar.

Print

6   Close the envelope document without saving it.

If You Want to Continue to the Next Lesson

▶ Be sure the Startup dialog box is open.

If You Want to Quit Works for Now

*Application
Control-menu box*

1   Click the Cancel button in the Startup dialog box.

2   Double-click the Application Control-menu box in the Microsoft Works title bar.

Lesson Summary

To	Do this	Button
Create a form letter	Open the Form Letter WorksWizard. Follow the directions and answer the questions that appear on screen, clicking the Next > button after you complete each step. When you have answered all the questions, click the Done button.	
Create mailing labels	Open a new Word Processor document, choose Envelopes And Labels from the Tools menu, and then click the Mailing Labels tab. Click the Fields>> button, click the Database button, and then select a database. In the Fields list box, select field names to insert placeholders in the Label text box, select a Label style, and then click the Create Label button.	
Create envelopes	Open a new Word Processor document and then choose Envelopes And Labels from the Tools menu. Click the Fields button, click the Database button, and then select a database. In the Fields list box, select field names to insert placeholders in the Address box, type a return address in the Return Address box, select an envelope size, and then click the Create Envelope button.	
Preview form letters, mailing labels, or envelopes	Click the Print Preview button on the toolbar, double-click the name of a database, and then click the OK button.	
Print a test row of mailing labels	From the File menu, choose Print, click the Test button, double-click the name of a database, and then click the OK button.	

To	Do this	Button
Print form letters, mailing labels, or envelopes	Click the Print button on the toolbar, double-click the name of a database, and then click the OK button.	
Address and print a single envelope	Open a new Word Processor document, choose Envelopes And Labels from the Tools menu, type a name and address in the Address box, type a return address in the Return Address box, and then click the Create Envelope button. Click the Print button on the toolbar.	

For more information on	See in the *Microsoft Works User's Guide*
Producing form letters	Chapter 3, "Creating form letters" Chapter 11, "Printing form letters"
Producing mailing labels	Chapter 11, "Printing mailing labels"
Producing envelopes	Chapter 11, "Printing envelopes"

For online information about	From the Help menu, choose Contents and then
Producing form letters	Choose "Word Processor," choose "Word Processor basics," and select the topic "Creating a form letter."
Producing mailing labels	Choose "Word Processor," choose "Word Processor basics," and select the topic "Creating a mailing label document."
Producing envelopes	Choose "Word Processor," choose "Word Processor basics," and select the topic "Printing envelopes."

Preview of the Next Lesson

In this lesson, you used a WorksWizard and the print merge feature to personalize and automate document creation. In the next lesson, you'll learn how to use Microsoft Draw, a tool that lets you insert lines, boxes, and drawings into your documents. You'll use drawing tools to draw lines and other shapes, and you'll insert a clip art drawing in a Word Processor document.

Getting Started with Microsoft Draw

The flyer that you created and worked with in the first three lessons was geared toward existing West Coast Sales customers. To attract new customers, you decide to create a second promotional flyer advertising your spring sale, to be used for a mass mailing. You've already typed the text portion of the flyer, and now you want to turn it into a really eye-catching document that will capture the attention of potential customers. You can accomplish this task easily because you have the perfect tool at your disposal: Microsoft Draw.

Microsoft Draw is a Works accessory that you can use to add artwork to your documents. You might use Microsoft Draw to design a company logo, create drawings to illustrate important points in a report, or draw lines that divide a document into sections. You can also use other features, like ClipArt and WordArt, to enhance your documents with professionally-designed pictures and special text effects.

In this lesson, you'll use artwork to enhance the mass mailing flyer announcing your spring video sale. First, you'll use Microsoft Draw to create a logo, and then you'll add clip art and a special text effect to your document.

If your screen does not match the illustrations in this lesson, see the Appendix, "Matching the Exercises."

You will learn how to:

- Create a drawing.
- Add clip art to a document.
- Use WordArt.

Estimated lesson time: 20 minutes

Start the lesson

1 In the Startup dialog box, click the Open An Existing Document button.

2 Make sure C:\MSWORKS\WORKSSBS is the current directory.

3 In the File Name list box, double-click ANNOUNCE.WPS.

Maximize

4 If the document doesn't fill the entire Word Processor window, click the Maximize button in the document window title bar.

Creating a Drawing

A drawing consists of one or more *objects*. A drawing object might be a rectangle, circle, line, arc, polygon, or block of text. To create a drawing, you open a document, position the insertion point at the location where you want the drawing, start Microsoft Draw, and use the drawing tools to draw objects. When your drawing is complete, you exit Microsoft Draw and insert the drawing in the document. In the next exercises, you'll use Microsoft Draw to create a logo for your flyer.

Start Microsoft Draw

Maximize

1   Press CTRL+END to position the insertion point at the bottom of the document.

2   From the Insert menu, choose Drawing.

    Microsoft Draw starts and opens the drawing window.

3   In the drawing window, click the Maximize button to maximize the drawing window.

    The components of the drawing window are listed in the following illustration.

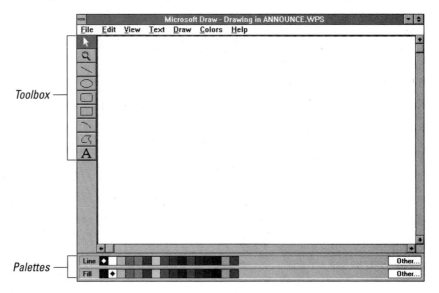

Draw objects

The drawing window contains a toolbox on the left side with nine drawing tools. To draw an object, you click a drawing tool, move the pointer into the drawing area, and drag the pointer.

Ellipse/Circle

1   Click the Ellipse/Circle tool in the toolbox.

2   Move the pointer into the center of the drawing area.

    The pointer appears in the shape of cross hairs ($+$).

3   Drag the pointer down about 1 inch and right about 2 1/2 inches, and then release the mouse button.

    Your drawing area should now contain an ellipse, similar to the one shown in the following illustration.

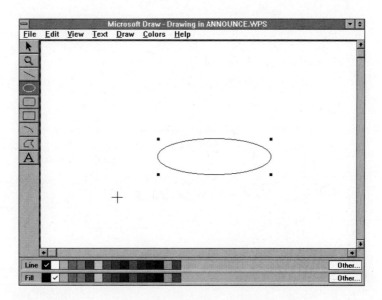

Note If your drawing does not match the illustration, you can press DELETE to delete the object, and then you can draw it again. You can also choose Undo from the Edit menu to delete the last object drawn.

*Rounded
Rectangle/Square*

4 Click the Rounded Rectangle/Square tool in the toolbox.

5 Draw a rectangle on top of the ellipse, as shown in the following illustration.

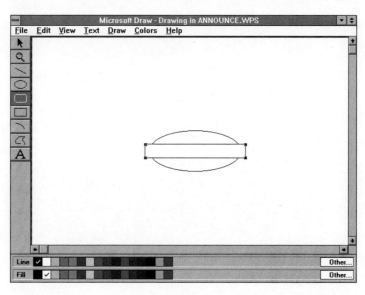

> **Tip**   With the rectangle tools, you can draw a perfect square by holding down SHIFT while you drag the mouse pointer. Likewise, you can use SHIFT with the Ellipse/Circle tool to draw a perfect circle.

Change the fill

There are two *palettes* at the bottom of the drawing window that you can use to change the colors and patterns of objects. You use the Line palette to change the color or pattern of lines and the borders of objects. You use the Fill palette to change an object's interior color or pattern.

Pointer

1   Click the Pointer tool in the toolbox.

2   In the drawing area, click the ellipse.

Small black squares called *handles* appear around the ellipse, indicating that it is selected. You must select an object before you can modify it.

3   Click the charcoal gray color box in the Fill palette.

The interior of the ellipse is now charcoal gray. The interior color of the rectangle remains white, providing a visible contrast between the objects.

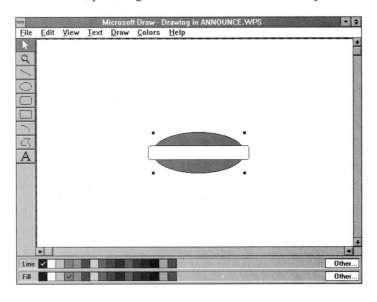

Add text

Your drawing doesn't have to be limited to basic shapes. You can enhance your logo by adding text.

Text

1   Click the Text tool in the toolbox.

2   In the drawing area, click inside the rectangle near the left border.

The text insertion point appears in the rectangle.

3   Type **Electronics - Music - Videos**

4   Press ENTER.

You'll need to modify the text to make it fit in the rectangle object.

Modify the text

1   Be sure handles appear around the text object. If they don't appear around the text object, click the text.

2   From the Text menu, choose Font, and then select Arial.

3   From the Text menu, choose Size, and then select 8.

4   From the Text menu, choose Bold.

5   Click a blank section of the drawing area to deselect the text object.

Your drawing should now look similar to the following illustration.

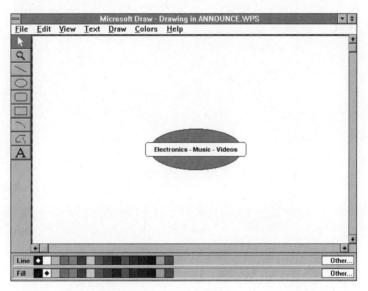

Tip   If your text object is not positioned where you want it, you can move it by clicking the text object and using the mouse to drag it to a new position.

Insert the drawing

Now that your logo is complete, you can easily insert it in your document.

1   From the File menu, choose Exit And Return To ANNOUNCE.WPS.

The following message box appears.

2   Click the Yes button to update ANNOUNCE.WPS.

The drawing is inserted into the document.

3   Scroll up until the drawing is at the bottom of the Word Processor window. Your document should look like the following illustration.

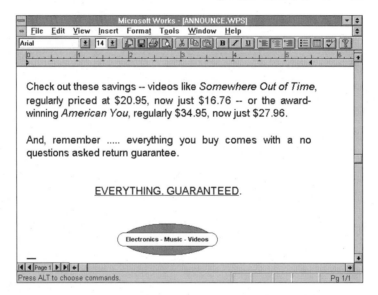

Adding Clip Art to a Document

Clip art is a collection of ready-made drawings and pictures. Works includes a ClipArt Gallery from which you can view and select clip art to insert in your documents. In the next exercises, you'll add a clip art picture above the company name at the top of your document.

Open the ClipArt Gallery

1   Press CTRL+HOME to position the insertion point at the top of the document.

2   From the Insert menu, choose ClipArt.

If this is the first time you have used clip art, the Microsoft ClipArt Gallery dialog box will appear. Click the Yes button in the Microsoft ClipArt Gallery dialog box to make the Add Clipart dialog box appear, as shown in the next illustration.

When Works has finished adding clip art pictures, the Microsoft ClipArt Gallery opens, as shown in the next illustration.

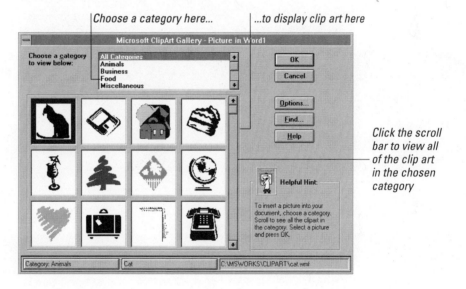

Note If you have used clip art prior to this exercise, the ClipArt Gallery will appear when you choose ClipArt from the Insert menu. You will not see the Add Clipart dialog box.

Insert and resize a clip art picture

1 In the Choose A Category To View Below list box, select Miscellaneous.

2 Scroll through the pictures and then double-click the Sun clip art picture.

   The clip art picture is inserted into the document, as shown in the next illustration.

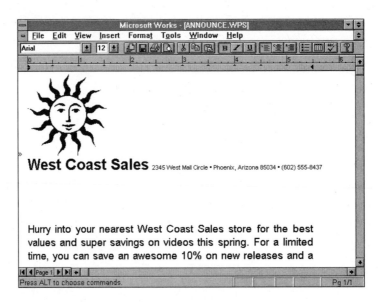

If the picture is too big or too small, you can resize it.

3 Click the clip art picture.

Small gray squares, called *sizing handles*, appear on the picture borders.

RESIZE

4 Position the pointer on the bottom right corner handle.

The pointer changes to the RESIZE pointer.

5 Drag the handle diagonally toward the top left corner about 1/2 inch to resize the picture, and then release the mouse button.

6 Click outside of the clip art picture.

Your document with the clip art picture should now look like the following illustration.

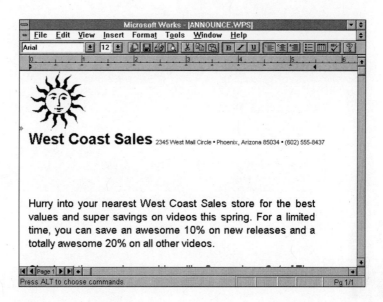

Using WordArt

WordArt is an accessory you can use to create text objects with special effects. Some of the effects available in WordArt include flipping and rotating text, printing text in a circle or half-circle, and adding shadows and borders to text.

You have chosen "Spring into Videos" as the catch phrase for your video promotion. In the next exercises, you'll use WordArt to apply a special text effect to the phrase and insert it into your document.

Start WordArt

1   Position the insertion point two lines above the first paragraph.

Center alignment has already been applied to the line.

2   From the Insert menu, choose WordArt.

The Enter Your Text Here dialog box appears.

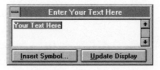

In the Enter Your Text Here dialog box you type the text to which you want to apply special effects.

Type the text

1   Type **Spring into Videos**

Control-menu box

2   In the Enter Your Text Here dialog box, double-click the Control-menu box.

The dialog box closes and the text appears in your document as an object with a shaded border. Notice that the toolbar now contains buttons you can use to apply special effects.

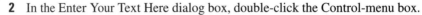

Special effects buttons

Apply special effects

Shape list box

1   Click the arrow to the right of the Shape list box on the toolbar.

The Shape list appears.

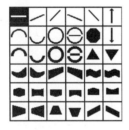

From the Shape list, you can select the angle or curve in which you want the text to appear.

2   Click the Wave 1 shape (the fourth shape down in the fifth column).

The wave effect is applied to the text. This effect will be more effective if you make the text larger.

| Best Fit |

Font Size list box

3   Click the arrow to the right of the Font Size list box on the toolbar.

4   Select 30.

The Size Change dialog box appears, asking you to confirm that you want to resize the WordArt object.

5 Click the Yes button to resize the WordArt object.

6 Click the Shadow button on the toolbar.

Shadow

The Shadow box appears.

7 In the third column, click the second shadow option.

The Size Change dialog box appears again because adding a shadow to the text makes it larger.

8 Click the Yes button to resize the WordArt object.

9 Click twice outside of the WordArt object.

Print Preview

10 Click the Print Preview button on the toolbar and then zoom in to preview the flyer.

Your screen should now look like the following illustration.

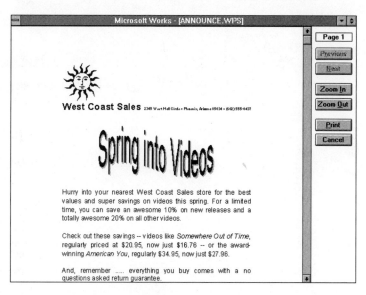

11 Click the Print button to print the flyer.

12 Save ANNOUNCE.WPS.

One Step Further

In this lesson, you inserted a clip art picture in your flyer document. What if you decide you would rather have a different clip art picture at the top of your document? You can easily replace the current picture with a different one from the ClipArt Gallery.

Replace the clip art picture

1   Double-click the Sun clip art picture.

The Microsoft ClipArt Gallery opens.

2   Double-click the Sailboat clip art picture.

The Sailboat replaces the Sun clip art picture. Again, you'll need to resize the object.

3   Drag the bottom right sizing handle until the clip art picture is about 1 inch square.

Save

4   Click the Save button on the toolbar to save your work.

If You Want to Continue to the Next Lesson

*Document
Control-menu box*

▶ Double-click the Document Control-menu box in the menu bar to close ANNOUNCE.WPS.

If You Want to Quit Works for Now

*Application
Control-menu box*

▶ Double-click the Application Control-menu box in the title bar.

Lesson Summary

To	Do this	Button
Start Microsoft Draw	Open a document and then choose Drawing from the Insert menu.	
Change the fill of an object	Select the object and then click a color box in the Fill palette.	
Add text to a drawing	Click the Text tool in the toolbox, click in the drawing area, and then type the text.	A
Change the font of a text object	Select the text object, choose Font from the Text menu, and then select a font.	
Change the font size of a text object	Select the text object, choose Size from the Text menu, and then select a size.	
Change the font style of a text object	Select the text object and then choose Bold, Italic, or Underline from the Text menu.	
Insert a clip art picture	From the Insert menu, choose ClipArt, and then double-click a picture in the ClipArt Gallery.	
Replace a clip art picture	Double-click the clip art picture in the document and then double-click a new picture in the ClipArt Gallery.	

To	Do this
Insert WordArt text	From the Insert menu, choose WordArt, type the text, close the Enter Your Text Here dialog box, and then use the toolbar to apply special effects.
Resize an object	Click the object and then drag a sizing handle.

For more information on	See in the *Microsoft Works User's Guide*
Creating drawings	Chapter 9, "Creating and modifying a drawing"
Adding clip art to documents	Chapter 9, "Adding clip art to a document"
Using WordArt	Chapter 10, "Creating special text effects with WordArt"

For online information about	From the Help menu, choose Contents and then
Creating drawings	Select the topic "Getting Help on Microsoft Draw."
Adding clip art to documents	Choose "Word Processor," choose "Changing Word Processor information," and select the topic "Inserting ClipArt objects in the Word Processor and Database."
Using WordArt	Choose "Word Processor," choose "Changing Word Processor information," and select the topic "Inserting WordArt objects in the Word Processor and Database."

Preview of the Next Lessons

In Part 2 of this book, you'll learn how to use the Spreadsheet tool. In Lesson 5, you'll learn the basics of creating, editing, and printing a spreadsheet. In Lesson 6, you'll learn about formatting features that will make your spreadsheets attractive and easy to read. In Lesson 7, you'll learn how to create, modify, and print charts of spreadsheet data.

Review & Practice

In the lessons in Part 1, "Using the Word Processor," you learned skills that will help you create professional looking text documents, as well as produce form letters, mailing labels, and envelopes to give your documents a personal touch. You also learned how to add drawings, clip art, and special text effects to your documents. If you want to practice these skills and test your understanding before you move on to the lessons in Part 2, you can work through the Review & Practice section following this lesson.

Part 1   Review & Practice

Before you move on to working with the Spreadsheet, you can practice the skills you learned in Part 1 by working through this Review & Practice section.

Scenario

As the office manager for a new branch of West Coast Sales, you are responsible for a variety of administrative duties. Your company has recently opened a new store and you need to produce a letter notifying your customers of the new location. You decide to create a letter that contains the new store address and some promotional information about the company. You also want to include some artwork and use the company's client database to produce personalized form letters and envelopes.

You will review and practice how to:

- Open and edit a document.
- Format a document.
- Set tabs and type a table.
- Add clip art to a document.
- Produce form letters and envelopes.

Estimated practice time: 25 minutes

Step 1: Open and Edit a Document

In this step, you'll open an existing document and edit it to create the letter announcing your new branch location. You'll find and replace text, check the spelling of the document, find a synonym, and move a paragraph.

Open a document

▶ Open NEWWEST.WPS from the C:\MSWORKS\WORKSSBS directory.

Find and replace text

1 Open the Replace dialog box.

2 Replace all occurrences of "stereo" with "audio."

3 Close the Replace dialog box.

Check the spelling of a document

1 Click the Spelling Checker button.

2   Correct each misspelled word in the document.

Find a synonym

1   In the last sentence of the letter, highlight the word "helping."

2   Open the Thesaurus dialog box.

3   Change "helping" to "assisting."

Move a paragraph

1   Highlight the paragraph that begins "Free delivery and set up..." and the blank line below it.

2   Drag the highlighted paragraph to the left of the paragraph that begins "A one-year guarantee...."

3   Save the file as NEWWEST1.WPS.

For more information on	See
Opening a document	Lesson 1
Finding and replacing text	Lesson 2
Checking spelling	Lesson 2
Finding a synonym	Lesson 2
Moving a paragraph	Lesson 2

Step 2: Format a Document

In this step, you'll improve the appearance of the document by changing margins; changing the font, size, and style of text; changing alignment; and adding bullets to paragraphs.

Change margins

1   Open the Page Setup dialog box and then click the Margins tab if it is not the displayed tab.

2   Set 2-inch top and bottom margins and 1.5-inch left and right margins.

Change the font and size of text

1   Hold down CTRL and click in the left margin to highlight all text in the document.

2   Change the font to Arial.

3   Change the font size to 10.

Change the style of text

1   Highlight the paragraph that begins "Free delivery and set up...."

2   Italicize the highlighted text.

Change the alignment of text

1 Highlight all text in the document.

2 Open the Paragraph dialog box and then click the Indents And Alignment tab.

3 Change the alignment to Justified.

Add bullets to paragraphs

1 Drag the pointer from the beginning of the paragraph that begins "Free delivery and set up..." to the end of the paragraph that begins "A money-back guarantee...."

2 Click the Bullets button on the toolbar to add bullets to the paragraphs.

For more information on	See
Changing margins	Lesson 2
Changing the font, size, and style of text	Lesson 2
Changing the alignment of text	Lesson 2
Adding bullets	Lesson 2

Step 3: Set Tabs and Type a Table

In this step, you'll set tabs, type a table, change tab alignment, and change line spacing.

Set tabs

1 Position the insertion point on the blank line below the paragraph that begins "Each West Coast Sales location..." and then press ENTER.

2 Click below the 1 inch mark and the 4 inch mark on the ruler to insert two tab stops.

Type a table

1 Type the following table. Press TAB before each entry, and press SHIFT+ENTER after each line to make the table a single paragraph.

Videolux mini camcorder	**$999.00**
Kennington KXP-2000 stereo	**1,489.99**
Mighty View 19" stereo TV	**349.99**

2 Insert a blank line below the table.

Change tab alignment

1 Highlight the table.

2 Open the Tabs dialog box and change the alignment of the 4 inch tab to Decimal.

Change line spacing

1 Open the Paragraph dialog box and then click the Breaks And Spacing tab.

2 Change the line spacing between lines to 1.25.

3 Save NEWWEST1.WPS.

4 Close NEWWEST1.WPS and return to the Startup dialog box.

For more information on	See
Setting tabs	Lesson 2
Typing a table	Lesson 2
Changing tab alignment	Lesson 2
Changing line spacing	Lesson 2

Step 4: Produce Form Letters and Envelopes

In this step, you'll create your form letters and envelopes. You'll use a WorksWizard, insert placeholders, preview and print the form letters, create envelopes, and preview and print the envelopes.

Start the WorksWizard

1 Start the Form Letter WorksWizard.

2 Use the NEWWEST1.WPS document and the WCCLIENT.WDB database.

Insert placeholders

1 Insert the following placeholders at the top of the document:

<<First Name>> <<Last Name>>
<<Address>>
<<City>>, <<State>> <<Zip>>

Dear <<First Name>>:

2 Complete the WorksWizard without sorting the letters.

Preview and print form letters

1 Click the Print Preview button.

2 Double-click WCCLIENT.WDB in the Choose Database dialog box to merge all the records.

3 Click the Print button.

4 Double-click WCCLIENT.WDB in the Choose Database dialog box to merge all the records.

5 Save NEWWEST1.WPS as NEWWEST2.WPS, and then close NEWWEST2.WPS.

6 Close WCCLIENT.WDB.

Create envelopes

1 Open a new Word Processor document.

2 Open the Envelopes And Labels dialog box and then click the Envelopes tab if it isn't the displayed tab.

3 Click the Fields>> button and then click the Database button.

4 Double-click WCCLIENT.WDB in the Choose Database dialog box and then click the OK button.

5 From the Fields box, insert the following placeholders in the Address box:

<<First Name>> <<Last Name>>
<<Address>>
<<City>>, <<State>> <<Zip>>

6 Type the following text in the Return Address box:

West Coast Sales
2500 Northwest Grand Avenue
Phoenix, Arizona 85006

7 Click the Create Envelope button.

Preview and print envelopes

1 Click the Print Preview button.

2 Select the WCCLIENT.WDB database and then merge all records.

3 Click the Print button.

4 Select the WCCLIENT.WDB database and then merge all records.

5 Close the envelope document without saving it.

For more information on	See
Creating a form letter	Lesson 3
Inserting placeholders	Lesson 3
Previewing and printing form letters	Lesson 3
Creating envelopes	Lesson 3
Previewing and printing envelopes	Lesson 3

Step 5: Add Clip Art to a Document

In this step, you'll insert and resize a clip art picture.

Insert a clip art picture

1 Open NEWWEST2.WPS.

2 Add a blank line at the top of the document and then move the insertion point to the blank line.

3 From the Insert menu, display the ClipArt Gallery.

4 Insert the Globe clip art picture.

Resize a clip art picture

1 Click the Globe clip art picture.

2 Drag the bottom right sizing handle until the picture is about 3/4 inch square.

3 Save NEWWEST2.WPS as NEWWEST3.WPS, and then close NEWWEST3.WPS.

For more information on	See
Inserting a clip art picture	Lesson 4
Resizing a clip art picture	Lesson 4

If You Want to Continue to the Next Lesson

▶ Be sure the Startup dialog box is open.

If You Want to Quit Works for Now

1 In the Startup dialog box, click the Cancel button.

2 Double-click the Application Control-menu box in the Microsoft Works title bar.

Part

2 Using the Spreadsheet

Getting Started with the Spreadsheet

The Spreadsheet is a versatile tool you can use to manage a home budget, develop a bookkeeping system and maintain records, or create complex business forecasts and projections. You can use the Spreadsheet to make simple or complex calculations. In addition to making calculations, you can use Spreadsheet editing and formatting features to easily revise data and create professional looking, easy to read documents.

The accounting department at West Coast Sales has provided you with sales, cost, and expense data that you are to use to analyze the video department's performance for the first quarter of the year. The previous department manager created a Spreadsheet document for this purpose and entered some of the information before being promoted to another department. Now that you are the department manager, you'll need to learn how to use the Works Spreadsheet tool so you can complete the existing spreadsheet and create other spreadsheets of your own.

In this lesson, you'll learn the basics of creating, editing, and printing spreadsheets.

If your screen does not match the illustrations in this lesson, see the Appendix, "Matching the Exercises."

You will learn how to:

- Start the Spreadsheet and open a document.
- Enter data in cells.
- Edit cell entries.
- Copy and move cell entries.
- Preview and print a spreadsheet.

Estimated lesson time: 20 minutes

Start the lesson

▶ Be sure the Startup dialog box is open.

Creating a Spreadsheet

A spreadsheet is a grid of columns and rows, similar to a ledger sheet used by an accountant. A spreadsheet contains 256 columns, labeled with letters, and 16,384 rows, labeled with numbers. The area formed by the intersection of a column and a row is called a *cell*. Each cell has a unique *cell reference*, which consists of the *column label* and *row number*. For example, the reference for the cell at the intersection of column A and row 1 is A1.

You create a spreadsheet by entering information in cells. A rectangular border in the spreadsheet, called the *highlight*, shows you the cell in which the next entry you type will be stored. The cell reference of the highlighted cell appears in the formula bar. The major components of a spreadsheet are shown in the following illustration.

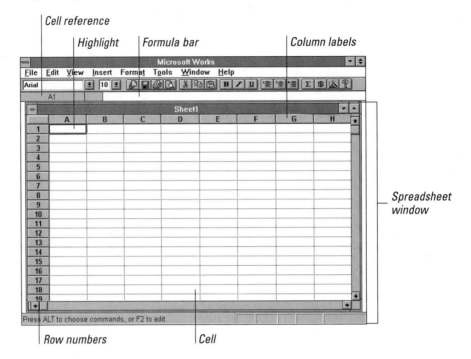

In the next exercises, you'll enter information in the spreadsheet that you will use to analyze the sales performance of your video department. You'll start the Spreadsheet tool, open the spreadsheet, enter data, and save the spreadsheet.

Start the Spreadsheet

Spreadsheet

▶ In the Startup dialog box, click the Spreadsheet button.

The Spreadsheet starts and opens a new spreadsheet window. Since you already have a partially completed spreadsheet to work with, you will open it instead of starting a new spreadsheet.

Open an existing spreadsheet

To create a new spreadsheet, you would use the spreadsheet window that opens when you click the Spreadsheet button in the Startup dialog box.

When you installed the practice files in the "Getting Ready" section, the files were copied to your hard disk and stored in the C:\MSWORKS\WORKSSBS directory. To locate and access the files, you must make the directory in which they are stored the current directory.

1   From the File menu, choose Open Existing File.

The Open dialog box appears, as shown in the following illustration.

Current directory

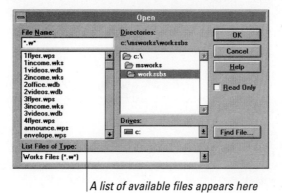

Selected directories

Click here to scroll down to the WORKSSBS folder icon

To make C:\MSWORKS\WORKSSBS the current directory, you must select each of the component directories (C:\, MSWORKS, and WORKSSBS). To select a directory, you double-click the corresponding folder icon. When a directory is selected, its icon appears as an open folder.

Note   If the C:\ and MSWORKS folder icons are already open, C:\MSWORKS is the current directory. If this is the case, you can skip to step 3.

2   In the Directories list box, double-click the C:\ folder icon and then double-click the MSWORKS folder icon to make C:\MSWORKS the current directory.

3   Scroll down in the Directories list box and then double-click the WORKSSBS folder icon to open the directory in which the practice files are stored.

Now that you have selected the WORKSSBS directory, a list of available files appears in the File Name list box, as shown in the following illustration.

A list of available files appears here

4   In the File Name list box, double-click 1INCOME.WKS.

The file opens.

5   Click the Maximize button in the 1INCOME.WKS title bar to make the document fill the entire window.

Maximize

Entering Data

To enter data in a spreadsheet, you move the highlight to a cell using the mouse or the arrow keys, type the data, and then press ENTER or an arrow key to complete the entry. The types of data you can enter in spreadsheet cells are text, numbers, formulas, series, and functions.

In the next exercises, you'll enter data and save the spreadsheet.

Enter text

You use text in a spreadsheet to provide descriptive labels for rows and columns or to give instructions.

1   Press the DOWN ARROW key.

The highlight moves to cell A2.

2   Type **Revenue Analysis** and then press ENTER.

The text appears in cell A2 and in the formula bar. The quotation mark that appears in the formula bar denotes the entry as a text entry.

3   Click cell A4.

The highlight moves to cell A4.

4   Type **Sales** and then press the DOWN ARROW key.

The text appears in cell A4 and the highlight moves down to cell A5.

5   Type **Cost** and then press ENTER.

Enter numbers

You use numbers in a spreadsheet to make calculations. Numeric entries can be whole numbers (such as 1 or 256), decimals (such as .5 or 8.27), fractions (such as 1 1/2), dates (such as 12/25/95), or times (such as 10:32 AM). The Sales, Cost, and Expenses data for January and February has already been entered in columns B and C. You will enter the data for March in column D.

1   Click cell D4.

2   Type **25120** and then press the DOWN ARROW key.

3   Type **10920** and then press ENTER.

4   Press the DOWN ARROW key three times to move the highlight to cell D8.

5   Type **5966** and then press ENTER.

Enter a series

To clarify the entries in your spreadsheet, you decide to add the name of the month that corresponds to each column of data. You can quickly enter a series of numbers or dates that automatically increase or decrease by a specified increment.

1   Move the highlight to cell B3.

2   Type **jan** and then press ENTER.

"January" appears in cell B3. This is a numeric date entry. You can use it to fill the adjoining cells with an increasing or decreasing series of dates.

Note   You can also enter the name of a month as a text entry, which is simply text, and cannot be used to enter a series. To do this, you must precede the entry with a quotation mark (for example, "January).

---

3   Position the pointer over cell B3.

4   Hold down the mouse button, drag the pointer to cell D3, and then release the mouse button.

Dragging across a range of cells highlights those cells. You've just highlighted the range B3 through D3. You highlight a range when you want to apply a command or an action to two or more adjacent cells.

Highlighted range

	A	B	C	D	E	F	G	H	
1	West Coast Sales								
2	Revenue Analysis								
3		January			Totals	Averages			
4	Sales	24080	27760	25120					
5	Cost	9030	12705	10920	32655				
6									
7	Gross Profit				0				
8	Expenses	6020	9022	5966	21008				
9									
10	Revenue								
11									

5   From the Edit menu, choose Fill Series.

The Fill Series dialog box appears.

6   Under Units, select Month, as shown in the following illustration.

Select Month ——— 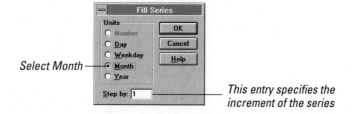 ——— *This entry specifies the increment of the series*

7   Click the OK button.

The highlighted cells are filled with a series of dates that increment by one month.

Tip   To enter a decreasing series, change the Step By entry in the Fill Series dialog box to a negative number.

Your spreadsheet should now look like the following illustration.

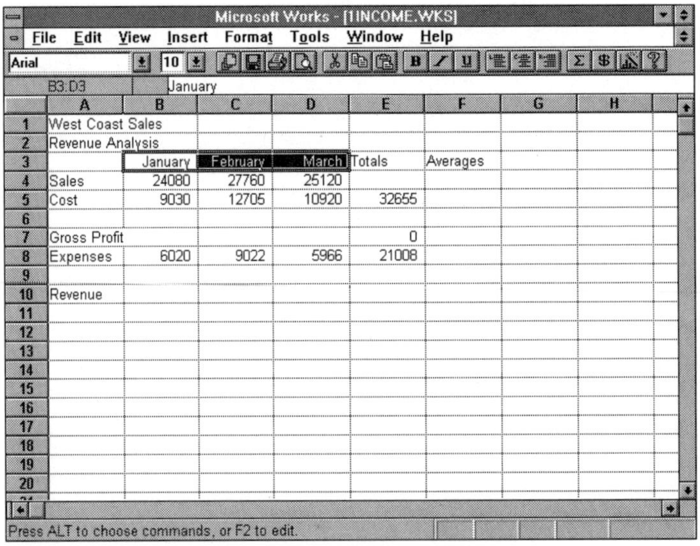

Enter formulas

You use formulas to perform calculations on numbers that already exist in a spreadsheet. Formulas must begin with an equal sign (=) and can contain numbers, cell references, other formulas, and mathematical operators (such as +, -, *, or /).

You need to enter two formulas in your spreadsheet to calculate Gross Profit and Revenue. Gross Profit is Sales minus Cost; Revenue is Gross Profit minus Expenses. You can type an entire formula from the keyboard or you can move the highlight to add cell references to a formula.

1   Move the highlight to cell B7.

2   Type **=b4-b5** and then press ENTER.

Works subtracts the number in cell B5 (Cost) from the number in cell B4 (Sales). The result of the formula (Gross Profit) appears in cell B7 and the formula appears in the formula bar, as shown in the following illustration.

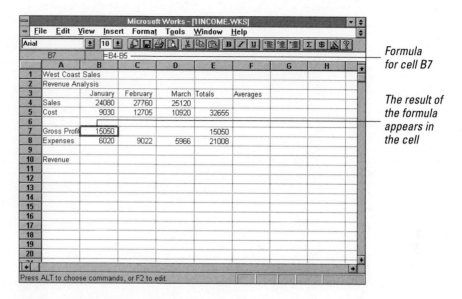

Formula for cell B7

The result of the formula appears in the cell

3   Move the highlight to cell B10.

Now you'll use the mouse to enter a formula to calculate Revenue.

4   Type = to begin the formula.

5   Click cell B7.

Works appends the cell reference to the entry in the formula bar.

6   Type –

The highlight moves back to the starting cell after you specify a mathematical operator.

7   Click cell B8 to append the cell reference to the entry in the formula bar.

8   Press ENTER to complete the Revenue formula.

Your spreadsheet should now look like the following illustration.

	A	B	C	D	E	F	G	H
1	West Coast Sales							
2	Revenue Analysis							
3		January	February	March	Totals	Averages		
4	Sales	24080	27760	25120				
5	Cost	9030	12705	10920	32655			
6								
7	Gross Profit	15050			15050			
8	Expenses	6020	9022	5966	21008			
9								
10	Revenue	9030						
11								

Microsoft Works - [1INCOME.WKS]
File Edit View Insert Format Tools Window Help
Arial   10
B10   =B7-B8

Press ALT to choose commands, or F2 to edit.

Enter functions

Functions are predefined formulas that perform special calculations. You can use functions for calculations such as totaling a column of numbers or calculating the future value of an investment.

Functions begin with an equal sign, followed by a word or abbreviation that defines the action of the function. Most functions require *arguments*, which are numbers, cell references, or text that are used to make the required calculations.

Works contains 76 functions that you can use in your spreadsheets. Two of these functions are the AVG and SUM functions, which you'll use to calculate a sales average and a sales total.

1 Move the highlight to cell F4.

2 Type **=avg(b4:d4)**

The range reference in parentheses is the argument. It specifies the starting and ending cell of the range for which you want to average the numbers. You must separate the cell references in the argument with a colon (:).

3 Press ENTER.

The AVG function averages the numbers in the specified range of cells.

4 Move the highlight to cell E4.

5 Click the Autosum button on the toolbar.

Autosum

Works inserts the SUM function in the formula bar and highlights an adjacent range of cells containing numbers. The SUM function will total the numbers in the highlighted range of cells. Your spreadsheet should match the following illustration.

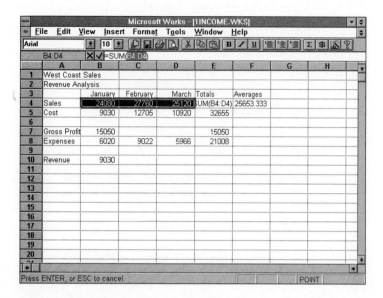

Enter box

6 Click the Enter box on the formula bar.

Works inserts the SUM function in the cell and totals the highlighted numbers. Your spreadsheet should now match the following illustration.

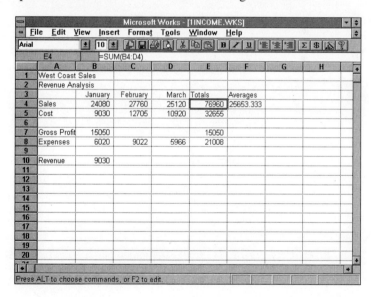

Note Clicking the Enter box is just like pressing the ENTER key when you're done making a cell entry.

Save the spreadsheet

As you create or change a spreadsheet, your work is held in the computer's temporary memory. To ensure that you don't lose data, you should save your spreadsheet periodically.

1 From the File menu, choose Save As.

The Save As dialog box appears with the current filename highlighted in the File Name text box.

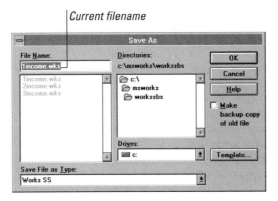

Current filename

2 Type **income1** in the File Name text box and then press ENTER.

The spreadsheet has now been saved as INCOME1.WKS, as indicated in the spreadsheet title bar. The original file, 1INCOME.WKS, is left in its original form.

Editing a Spreadsheet

As you review the data you received from the accounting department, you realize that some of the information that was previously entered into your spreadsheet is now outdated. You also see that you still need to make a few calculations.

The Spreadsheet has a wide range of editing capabilities that you can use to make changes to a spreadsheet. You can easily replace all or part of a cell entry with new data, clear data from a cell or range, and copy or move data from one cell to another.

In the next exercises, you'll edit your spreadsheet to reflect the current accounting figures, remove unnecessary information, and copy and move cell entries.

Replace a cell entry

You need to replace the Sales number for January.

1 Move the highlight to cell B4.

2 Type **23885** and then press ENTER.

The new entry replaces the entire cell entry. The formulas you previously entered in cells B7 and B10 are automatically recalculated when you change the entry in cell B4. Formulas that contain cell references are automatically recalculated when you change the numbers in the referenced cells.

Edit a cell entry

The Expenses number for February is also incorrect; however, you need to change only one digit in the number. You can use EDIT mode instead of replacing the entire entry.

1 Move the highlight to cell C8.

2 Click to the right of the number in the formula bar.

Clicking the formula bar turns on EDIT mode. An insertion point and the contents of the cell now appear in the formula bar.

3 Press the LEFT ARROW key three times.

The insertion point moves left three characters in the formula bar.

4 Press DELETE to delete the character to the right of the insertion point.

Note   You can press BACKSPACE if you want to delete the character to the left of the insertion point.

---

5 Type **1** and then press ENTER.

The edited entry, 9122, now appears in cell C8. Your spreadsheet should now match the following illustration.

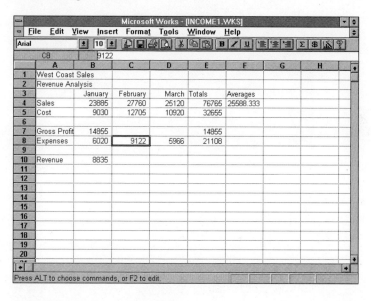

Clear cell entries

You decide that you don't need to show the averages for each row of data. You can delete this information by clearing the cell entries.

1 Drag the pointer across cells F3 and F4 to highlight the cells.

2 Press DELETE to clear the entries from the cells.

Copy cell entries

So far you've entered Gross Profit and Revenue formulas for January, but not for February and March. Instead of entering additional formulas, you can save time by copying the January formulas.

1 Move the highlight to cell B7.

Copy

2 Click the Copy button on the toolbar.

The formula is copied and stored in the Clipboard, which is a temporary storage area in the computer's memory.

3 Highlight cells C7 and D7.

Paste

4 Click the Paste button on the toolbar.

Works pastes the formula from the Clipboard into the highlighted cells.

5 Click cell D7.

The formula bar reads "=D4-D5." When you copy a formula, the cell references automatically adjust to reflect the new location of the formula.

6 Highlight cells B10 through D10.

7 From the Edit menu, choose Fill Right.

The formula in cell B10 is copied to the adjacent highlighted cells.

	A	B	C	D	E	F	G	H
1	West Coast Sales							
2	Revenue Analysis							
3		January	February	March	Totals			
4	Sales	23885	27760	25120	76765			
5	Cost	9030	12705	10920	32655			
6								
7	Gross Profit	14855	15055	14200	44110			
8	Expenses	6020	9122	5966	21108			
9								
10	Revenue	8835	5933	8234				
11								

Note You can choose Fill Down from the Edit menu if you want to copy vertically to adjacent cells.

DRAG

8 Click cell E4 and then position the pointer on a border of the cell.

The pointer changes to the DRAG pointer.

9 Hold down CTRL, drag the highlight to cell E10, and then release the mouse button and CTRL.

COPY

The pointer changes to the COPY pointer and the entry in cell E4 is copied to cell E10, as shown in the following illustration. This feature is called *drag-and-drop*.

	A	B	C	D	E	F	G	H	
1	West Coast Sales								
2	Revenue Analysis								
3		January	February	March	Totals				
4	Sales	23885	27760	25120	76765				
5	Cost	9030	12705	10920	32655				
6									
7	Gross Profit	14855	15055	14200	44110				
8	Expenses	6020	9122	5966	21108				
9									
10	Revenue	8835	5933	8234	23002				
11									

Move cell entries

You decide the titles at the top of the spreadsheet would look better centered over the data. You can use the drag-and-drop feature to move them.

1 Highlight cells A1 and A2.

2 Position the pointer on a border of the highlighted cells so that it appears as the DRAG pointer.

3 Drag the highlight to cells C1 and C2 and then release the mouse button.

The entries move to cells C1 and C2. Your spreadsheet should now look like the following illustration.

```
Microsoft Works - [INCOME1.WKS]
File  Edit  View  Insert  Format  Tools  Window  Help
Arial          10
     C1:C2              "West Coast Sales
```

	A	B	C	D	E	F	G	H	
1			West Coast Sales						
2			Revenue Analysis						
3		January	February	March	Totals				
4	Sales	23885	27760	25120	76765				
5	Cost	9030	12705	10920	32655				
6									
7	Gross Profit	14855	15055	14200	44110				
8	Expenses	6020	9122	5966	21108				
9									
10	Revenue	8835	5933	8234	23002				
11									
12									
13									
14									
15									
16									
17									
18									
19									
20									

Press ALT to choose commands.

Cut

Paste

Note   You can also use the Cut and Paste buttons on the toolbar to move cell entries.

Save

4 Click the Save button on the toolbar to save your work.

The spreadsheet is saved with its current name.

Printing a Spreadsheet

When you are satisfied with the accuracy and appearance of your spreadsheet, you can print it. You can preview the spreadsheet to see how it will look when printed. Previewing allows you to review the overall layout of a spreadsheet and spot any areas that require last minute changes. In the next exercises, you'll preview and print your spreadsheet.

Preview a spreadsheet before printing

Print Preview

1 Click the Print Preview button on the toolbar.

Your spreadsheet appears in the Print Preview window.

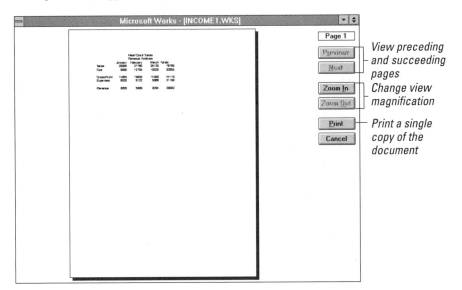

View preceding and succeeding pages

Change view magnification

Print a single copy of the document

If the data in the Print Preview window is too small for you to see, you can magnify the view.

2 Move the pointer over the data in the Print Preview window.

ZOOM

The pointer changes to the ZOOM pointer. When you click once, the view is magnified. Clicking a second time enlarges the view again. Clicking a third time returns the view to normal magnification, making the full page visible in the Print Preview window.

3 Click the data on the sample page twice to magnify the view.

4 Click the sample page a third time to shrink the view back to normal magnification.

Tip   You can also click the Zoom In and Zoom Out buttons to change the magnification of the view.

---

5   Click the Cancel button to close the Print Preview window.

Print a spreadsheet

1   From the File menu, choose Print.

The Print dialog box appears.

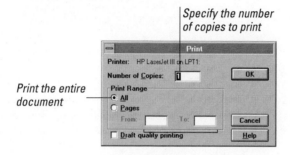

Specify the number of copies to print

Print the entire document

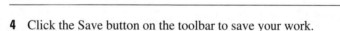

2   Type **2** in the Number Of Copies text box.

3   Click the OK button to print both copies of the spreadsheet.

Print

Save

Tip   You can click the Print button on the toolbar to print a spreadsheet using the current Print dialog box settings.

---

4   Click the Save button on the toolbar to save your work.

One Step Further

The word "Revenue" is a little fancier than you like, so you decide to replace it with "Income" throughout the spreadsheet. You can use the find and replace feature to quickly accomplish this task.

Find and replace cell entries

1   Click any cell in the spreadsheet.

When you highlight only one cell, Works will find and replace data throughout the entire spreadsheet.

2   From the Edit menu, choose Replace.

The Replace dialog box appears.

3   Type **revenue** in the Find What text box, press TAB to move to the Replace With text box, and then type **Income**

The Replace dialog box should now look like the following illustration.

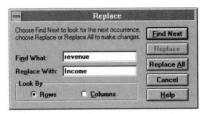

4 Click the Replace All button.

Works replaces all occurrences of "Revenue" with "Income."

Save

5 Click the Save button on the toolbar to save your work.

If You Want to Continue to the Next Lesson

*Document
Control-menu box*

1 Double-click the Document Control-menu box in the menu bar to close INCOME1.WKS.

2 Double-click the Document Control-menu box in the menu bar to close the empty spreadsheet window.

If You Want to Quit Works for Now

*Application
Control-menu box*

1 Close INCOME1.WKS and the empty spreadsheet window.

2 Choose Cancel in the Startup dialog box.

3 Double-click the Application Control-menu box in the Microsoft Works title bar.

Lesson Summary

To	Do this	Button
Start the Spreadsheet	Click the Spreadsheet button in the Startup dialog box.	
Open an existing spreadsheet	From the File menu, choose Open Existing File, and then double-click the name of the file you want to open in the File Name list box.	
Move the highlight from one cell to another	Press an arrow key or click a cell.	
Highlight a range of cells	Drag the pointer across the cells.	
Enter data in a cell	Move the highlight to the cell, type the data, and then press ENTER or an arrow key.	

To	Do this	Button
Enter a series	Enter the starting value in a cell, highlight the starting cell and the adjacent cells you want to fill with the series, choose Fill Series from the Edit menu, select a Units option, and then click the OK button.	
Save a spreadsheet	Click the Save button on the toolbar.	
Replace a cell entry	Move the highlight to the cell, type the new entry, and then press ENTER.	
Edit a cell entry	Move the highlight to the cell, click the formula bar, change the entry in the formula bar, and then press ENTER.	
Clear cell entries	Highlight the cells you want to clear, and then press DELETE.	
Copy cell entries	Highlight the cell entries you want to copy, click the Copy button on the toolbar, highlight the destination cells, and then click the Paste button on the toolbar. *or* Highlight the entries you want to copy, position the pointer on a border of the highlighted cells, and then hold down CTRL and drag the pointer to a new location.	
Copy a cell entry to adjacent cells	Highlight the cell that contains the entry you want to copy and the adjacent cells where you want to copy the entry. From the Edit menu, choose Fill Right or Fill Down.	
Move cell entries	Highlight the entries you want to move, position the pointer on a border of the highlighted cells, and then drag the highlighted entries to a new location.	
Preview a spreadsheet	Click the Print Preview button on the toolbar.	
Print a spreadsheet	Choose Print from the File menu, change print options, and then click the OK button. *or* Click the Print button on the toolbar.	

To	Do this
Find and replace cell entries	From the Edit menu, choose Replace, type the entry that you want to find, type the replacement entry, and then click the Replace All button.

For more information on	See in the *Microsoft Works User's Guide*
Entering data	Chapter 4, "Entering information" Chapter 4, "Entering text" Chapter 4, "Entering a number" Chapter 4, "Entering a formula" Chapter 4, "Using functions in formulas"
Saving a spreadsheet	Chapter 4, "Naming and saving a spreadsheet"
Editing a spreadsheet	Chapter 4, "Changing text, values, or formulas" Chapter 4, "Undoing changes" Chapter 4, "Copying and moving cell contents"
Finding and replacing cell entries	Chapter 4, "Finding and replacing specific text or values"
Printing a spreadsheet	Chapter 11, "Printing with Works"

For online information about	In the Help menu, choose Contents and then
Entering data	Choose "Spreadsheet," choose "Spreadsheet basics," and select the topic "Creating a spreadsheet."
Saving a spreadsheet	Choose "Works for Windows Basic Skills," choose "Working with documents," and select the topic "Saving a document."
Editing a spreadsheet	Choose "Spreadsheet," choose "Changing spreadsheet information," and select either "Changing an entry" or "Copying and moving information within the Spreadsheet."
Finding and replacing cell entries	Choose "Spreadsheet," choose "Spreadsheet basics," and select the topic "Replacing specific information in the Spreadsheet."
Printing a spreadsheet	Choose "Spreadsheet" and then choose "Printing a spreadsheet."

Preview of the Next Lesson

In this lesson, you opened your income analysis spreadsheet, entered data, changed some cell entries, and printed the spreadsheet. In the next lesson, you'll improve the appearance of your spreadsheet with a number of formatting features. You'll change the page orientation and margins, change column widths, insert rows and columns, change the appearance of numerical cell entries, change the alignment and font of cell entries, and add border lines and shading to groups of cells. You'll also use cell protection to prevent others from changing your spreadsheet data.

Formatting Spreadsheets

The income spreadsheet you created in the last lesson is accurate and contains all of the data you need to analyze the performance of your video department at West Coast Sales. Now upper management has asked you to submit a copy of your data for review, but you don't feel comfortable sending a copy of your spreadsheet in its current form. The data is somewhat difficult to read and could use more visual appeal. In this lesson, you'll use the Spreadsheet formatting features to improve the appearance of your spreadsheet.

If your screen does not match the illustrations in this lesson, see the Appendix, "Matching the Exercises."

You will learn how to:

- Change the page orientation and margins.
- Insert rows and columns.
- Change column widths.
- Change number formats.
- Change the alignment of cell entries.
- Change the font size and font style of text entries.
- Add borders and shading to cells.
- Protect cells from changes.

Estimated lesson time: 20 minutes

Start the lesson

1   In the Startup dialog box, click the Open An Existing Document button.

2   Make sure C:\MSWORKS\WORKSSBS is the current directory.

3   In the File Name list box, double-click 2INCOME.WKS.

   2INCOME.WKS contains more data, but otherwise matches the spreadsheet you worked with in Lesson 5.

Maximize

4   If the document doesn't fill the entire spreadsheet window, click the Maximize button in the spreadsheet window title bar.

Changing the Page Setup

You can markedly improve the appearance of your printed spreadsheet by changing the page setup, which controls the layout of the pages. Use the Page Setup command to change margins, the page orientation, and printing options. In the next exercises, you'll change the page setup to make your spreadsheet easier to read.

Change margins

Your spreadsheet data might look better centered horizontally on the page. You can adjust the left and right margins to center the data.

1   From the File menu, choose Page Setup.

The Page Setup dialog box appears showing margin options.

2   Double-click the Left Margin text box and then type **1.75**

3   Press TAB to move to the Right Margin text box, type **1.75**, and then press TAB.

The Sample section of the dialog box illustrates the new left and right margin settings you have specified.

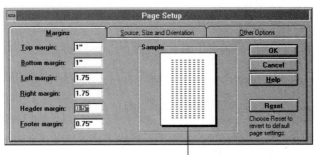

Sample of new
margin settings

Note   You can click the Reset button in the Page Setup dialog box to change the margins back to their original settings.

The new margin settings will not be applied to your spreadsheet until you click the OK button. Before you do that, however, you can specify new settings in other sections of the Page Setup dialog box and then apply all of the setting changes simultaneously.

Change the page orientation

Since your spreadsheet is now seven columns wide and the left and right margins are going to be larger than they were originally, the data would fit better if the page were turned horizontally. Horizontal page orientation would also provide extra space that you can use if you need to increase the width of columns.

1   Click the Source, Size And Orientation tab.

The current page orientation is portrait (vertical), as shown in the Sample section of the dialog box on the previous page.

2   Under Orientation, select Landscape.

The Sample section now illustrates landscape (horizontal) orientation.

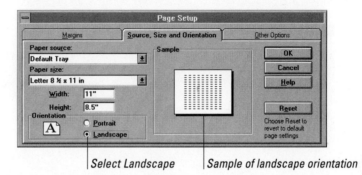

| Select Landscape | Sample of landscape orientation |

3   Click the OK button to apply the new margin and orientation settings.

Print Preview

4   Click the Print Preview button on the toolbar to view the new margins and the new page orientation.

Your spreadsheet in the Print Preview window should look like the next illustration.

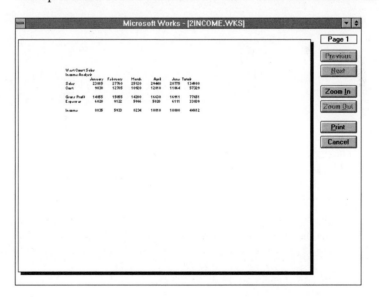

5   Click the Cancel button to close the Print Preview window.

Formatting Rows and Columns

The rows and columns of data in your income spreadsheet are rather close together and the spreadsheet is missing data for the month of May. You can take advantage of the new page setup to spread out your data by inserting some blank rows and widening the columns. You can add the data for May by inserting a new column and typing the necessary information. In the next exercises, you'll insert rows and columns, change column widths to make the spreadsheet easier to read, and add the missing data.

Insert rows

You can insert blank rows to increase the amount of space between the spreadsheet title and the month entries and between the month entries and the Sales data.

The row labels are the numbers that appear on the left side of the spreadsheet window.

1 Click the row label for row number 4 to highlight the entire row, as shown in the next illustration.

Click the row label to highlight the entire row

	A	B	C	D	E	F	G	H
1	West Coast Sales							
2	Income Analysis							
3		January	February	March	April	June	Totals	
4	Sales	23885	27760	25120	29440	28775	134980	
5	Cost	9030	12705	10920	12810	11864	57329	
6								
7	Gross Profit	14855	15055	14200	16630	16911	77651	
8	Expenses	6020	9122	5966	5820	6111	33039	
9								
10	Income	8835	5933	8234	10810	10800	44612	
11								

2 From the Insert menu, choose Row/Column.

Works inserts a new row above the highlighted row. The number of rows you highlight determines the number of rows that will be inserted.

3 Drag across row labels 3 and 4 to highlight the rows.

4 From the Insert menu, choose Row/Column.

Works inserts two new rows that separate the spreadsheet title from the rest of the spreadsheet. Your screen should look like the following.

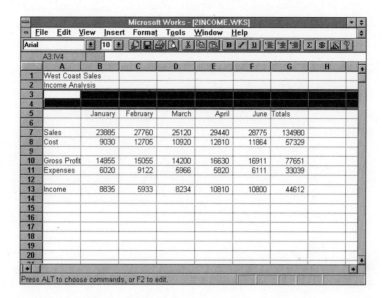

Insert a column

To make room for the May data, you'll need to insert a column.

1   Click column label F to highlight the entire column.

The number of columns you highlight determines the number of columns that will be inserted.

2   From the Insert menu, choose Row/Column.

Works inserts a new column to the left of the highlighted column. You can now enter the data for May in the new column.

Copy

Paste

3   Highlight cells G5 through G13 and then click the Copy button on the toolbar.

4   Move the highlight to cell F5 and then click the Paste button on the toolbar.

The data and formulas from cells G5 through G13 are copied to cells F5 through F13.

5   Change the entry in cell F5 to **May**

6   Change the entry in cell F7 to **31000**

7   Change the entry in cell F8 to **12468**

8   Change the entry in cell F11 to **5820**

Your spreadsheet should now match the following illustration.

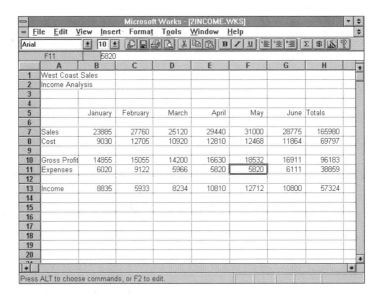

Change column widths

If cell entries are too long for the width of a column, or if you want to add space between columns, you can change column widths.

1   Drag across column labels B through H to highlight the columns.

Drag across column labels to highlight columns

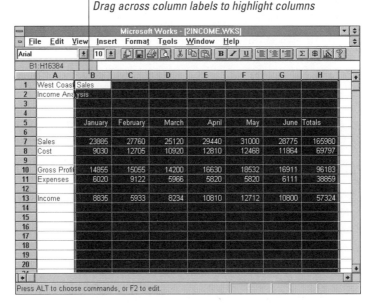

2 From the Format menu, choose Column Width.

The Column Width dialog box appears. Initially, all columns are preset to a width of 10 characters.

3 Type **12**

The Column Width dialog box should now appear as shown in the following illustration.

4 Press ENTER.

Columns B through H are now each 12 characters wide.

ADJUST

Tip You can also drag the border next to a column label to change the width of a column. When you place the pointer on the border, it changes to the ADJUST pointer.

5 Double-click column label A.

Works automatically adjusts the column to accommodate the width of the longest entry. This feature is called the *best fit*.

Tip You can also turn on the Best Fit check box in the Column Width dialog box to change a column width to the best fit.

Formatting Cells

You can make more detailed appearance changes to your spreadsheet by formatting cells individually or in groups. You can change number formats to make numbers easier to interpret, and you can change the font and alignment of cell entries and add borders and shading to make certain cell entries stand out from others. In the next exercises, you'll change number formats and enhance the appearance of your data.

Change number formats

1 Click the right horizontal scroll arrow until columns B through H are visible.

2 Highlight cells B7 through H7.

3 From the Format menu, choose Number.

The Number dialog box appears.

4 Under Format, select Currency.

The Currency format displays numbers with a leading dollar sign, thousands separators, and a specified number of decimals (numbers that appear to the right of the decimal point).

5 Type **0** to specify the number of decimals.

The Number dialog box should now look like the following illustration.

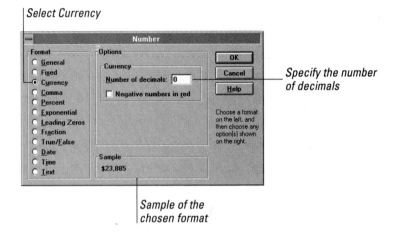

Select Currency

Specify the number of decimals

Sample of the chosen format

6 Press ENTER to apply the new number format.

The numbers in the highlighted cells now appear in the Currency format with no decimals. To avoid cluttering the spreadsheet with dollar signs, you will apply the Currency format to only the first and last rows of numbers.

7 Highlight cells B8 through H11.

8 From the Format menu, choose Number.

9 Under Format, select Comma.

The Comma format displays numbers with thousands separators and a specified number of decimals.

10 Type **0** to specify the number of decimals.

11 Press ENTER.

The numbers in the highlighted cells now appear in the Comma format with no decimals.

12 Highlight cells B13 through H13.

13 Click the Currency button on the toolbar.

Clicking the Currency button applies the Currency format with two decimals.

Currency

Change the alignment of cell entries

Your spreadsheet is looking better, but you can improve its readability even more by changing the alignment of certain cell entries. For example, the Totals label in cell H5 will be easier to see if it is right-aligned like the rest of the cell entries in row 5, and the Gross Profit and Income labels will be easier to locate if they are aligned differently than the rest of the cell entries in column A.

1   Move the highlight to cell H5.

Right Align

2   Click the Right Align button on the toolbar.

The cell entry aligns with the right border of the cell.

3   Move the highlight to cell A10.

Center Align

4   Click the Center Align button on the toolbar.

The entry is now centered in the cell.

5   Move the highlight to cell A13 and then click the Center Align button.

6   Highlight cells A1 through H2.

7   From the Format menu, choose Alignment.

The Alignment dialog box appears.

8   Under Alignment, select Center Across Selection.

The Alignment dialog box should now match the following illustration.

Select Center Across Selection

9   Click the OK button.

The cell entries are now centered within the highlighted block. Although the text appears to be in cells D1 through E2, it is actually the content of cell A1.

Change the font size and font style of text entries

You can make text entries stand out from the rest of the spreadsheet by changing the font size and the style of the text.

1   Move the highlight to cell A1.

Font Size list box

Bold

Italic

2 Click the arrow to the right of the Font Size list box on the toolbar and then select 16.

Selecting a larger font size makes the highlighted text larger.

3 Click the Bold button on the toolbar.

Now the spreadsheet title is large and bold.

4 Move the highlight to cell A2.

5 Click the Italic button on the toolbar.

The spreadsheet subtitle is now italicized, as shown in the next illustration.

Subtitle is italicized

Title is large and bold

	A	B	C	D	E	F	G
1				**West Coast Sales**			
2				*Income Analysis*			
3							
4							
5		January	February	March	April	May	
6							
7	Sales	$23,885	$27,760	$25,120	$29,440	$31,000	$2
8	Cost	9,030	12,705	10,920	12,810	12,468	1
9							
10	Gross Profit	14,855	15,055	14,200	16,630	18,532	1
11	Expenses	6,020	9,122	5,966	5,820	5,820	
12							
13	Income	$8,835.00	$5,933.00	$8,234.00	$10,810.00	$12,712.00	$10,8
14							

6 Highlight cells B5 through H5.

7 Click the Bold button on the toolbar to apply the bold style to the month headings.

8 Click cell H5.

Your spreadsheet should now match the next illustration.

	C	D	E	F	G	H	I
1		**West Coast Sales**					
2		*Income Analysis*					
3							
4							
5	February	March	April	May	June	Totals	
6							
7	$27,760	$25,120	$29,440	$31,000	$28,775	$165,980	
8	12,705	10,920	12,810	12,468	11,864	69,797	
9							
10	15,055	14,200	16,630	18,532	16,911	96,183	
11	9,122	5,966	5,820	5,820	6,111	38,859	
12							
13	$5,933.00	$8,234.00	$10,810.00	$12,712.00	$10,800.00	$57,324.00	
14							
15							
16							
17							
18							
19							
20							

Microsoft Works - [2INCOME.WKS]

File Edit View Insert Format Tools Window Help

Arial   10

H5   "Totals

Press ALT to choose commands, or F2 to edit.

Add borders

Adding borders will further differentiate the Cost, Expenses, and Income sections of your spreadsheet.

1 Highlight cells B8 through H8.

2 From the Forma**t** menu, choose **B**order.

The Border dialog box appears.

3 Under Border, select Botto**m**.

4 Under Line Style, select the third line style from the top.

The Border dialog box should now match the following illustration.

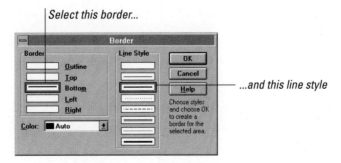

Select this border...

...and this line style

5 Click the OK button.

A border now appears along the bottom of each highlighted cell. You can see it if you click somewhere else on the spreadsheet to move the highlight.

6 Highlight cells B11 through H11.

7 From the Format menu, choose Border.

8 Under Border, select Bottom.

9 Under Line Style, select the third line style from the top, and then click the OK button.

10 Highlight cells B13 through H13.

11 From the Format menu, choose Border.

12 Under Border, select Bottom.

13 Under Line Style, select the sixth line style from the top, which is the double line, and then click the OK button.

Now it's easy to differentiate the sections of the spreadsheet.

14 Press CTRL+HOME to quickly move the pointer to cell A1.

Your spreadsheet should match the next illustration.

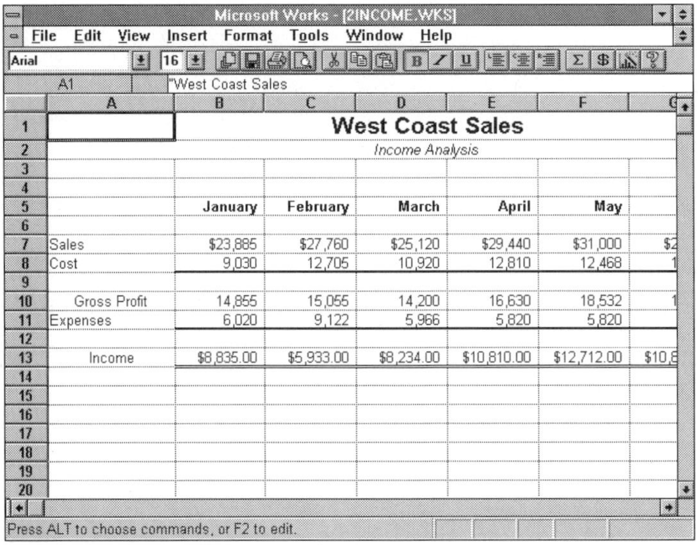

Add shading

You can make the column labels really stand out by adding shading to them.

1 Highlight cells A5 through H5.

2 From the Format menu, choose Patterns.

The Patterns dialog box appears.

3 Under Shading, click the arrow to the right of the Pattern list box.

4 Select the second shading pattern from the bottom.

The Patterns dialog box should now look like the following.

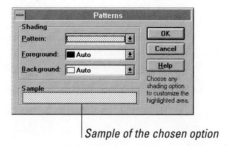

Sample of the chosen option

5   Click the OK button.

The highlighted cells are now shaded.

Hide and display gridlines

Gridlines are the horizontal and vertical lines that separate the rows and columns on a spreadsheet. While you are creating and editing a spreadsheet, gridlines are useful guides for locating cells. However, when your spreadsheet is complete, you may find it easier to read if you hide the gridlines.

1   Press CTRL+HOME to move the highlight to cell A1.

2   From the View menu, choose Gridlines to hide the gridlines.

Your spreadsheet should now look like the following illustration.

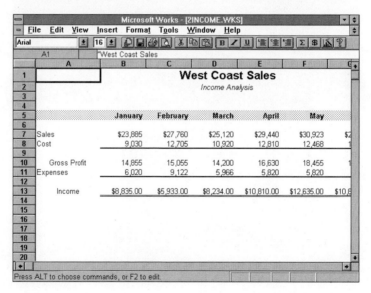

Note   You can print the spreadsheet with the gridlines hidden.

Since you have a bit more work to do before your spreadsheet is complete, you will redisplay the gridlines.

3   From the View menu, choose Gridlines to turn on the gridlines.

4   Save the spreadsheet as INCOME2.WKS.

Using Cell Protection

Spreadsheet files that are used by more than one person are at risk of being changed by accident or by unauthorized people. You can use *locked cells* and *cell protection* to prevent other users from changing or deleting cell entries.

Cells are protected from changes when they are locked and cell protection is turned on. Initially, all cells in a spreadsheet are locked and cell protection is turned off. Since cell protection isn't on, you can change or delete any cell entry. To protect some cells from changes while allowing changes to others, you must unlock those cells in which you will allow changes and then turn on cell protection to protect all of the other cells in the spreadsheet. In the next exercises, you'll use cell protection to prevent unauthorized changes to your spreadsheet data.

Unlock cells

Since the Sales, Cost, and Expenses data is subject to change, you decide to unlock the cells containing that data. Since the Gross Profit and Income data is based on calculations and doesn't require editing, you choose to keep the cells pertaining to that data locked.

1   Highlight cells B7 through G8.

2   From the Format menu, choose Protection.

The Protection dialog box appears.

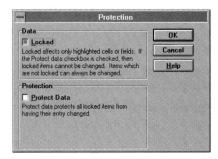

The highlighted cells are locked but not protected. Notice that the Locked check box is shaded. You must click once to turn the check box on; you click again to turn it off.

3   Under Data, click the Locked check box twice to turn it off, and then click the OK button.

The highlighted cells are now unlocked.

4 Highlight cells B11 through G11.

5 From the Format menu, choose Protection.

6 Turn off the Locked check box and then click the OK button.

Turn on cell protection

Now that you have unlocked the cells to which you will allow changes, you must turn on cell protection to protect the rest of the spreadsheet.

1 From the Format menu, choose Protection.

2 Under Protection, turn on the Protect Data check box, and then click the OK button.

The locked cells are now protected from changes or deletions. However, you can still change or delete the entries in the unlocked cells.

3 Move the highlight to cell A8.

4 Type **Cost of Goods** and then press ENTER.

Since cell A8 is locked, the following message box appears.

5 Click the OK button to close the message box.

6 Move the highlight to cell F7.

7 Type **30923** and then press ENTER.

Since the cell is unlocked, you can change the entry.

Save

8 Click the Save button on the toolbar to save your work.

One Step Further

Your spreadsheet looks great, but it doesn't identify the data as belonging to the video department. You can enter text in a cell to make this identification or you can create a *header*, which is a line of information that prints at the top of every page of a spreadsheet.

Create a header

You must turn off cell protection before you can create the header.

1 From the Format menu, choose Protection.

2 Under Protection, turn off the Protect Data check box, and then click the OK button.

3 From the View menu, choose Headers And Footers.

The Headers And Footers dialog box appears.

For a complete list of special codes that you can use in headers or footers, see the Microsoft Works User's Guide, *Chapter 4, "Creating headers and footers and numbering pages."*

4 Type **&lVideo Department&r&d**

This header will print the text "Video Department," left-aligned and the current date, right-aligned. The Headers And Footers dialog box should now look like the following.

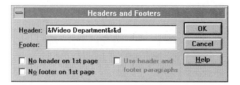

Note The character you type after the first ampersand (&) is a lowercase "L," not the number 1.

5 Press ENTER.

6 Click the Print Preview button on the toolbar to view the header.

Print Preview

7 Click the Print button in the Print Preview window to print the spreadsheet.

8 Save your work.

If You Want to Continue to the Next Lesson

Document Control-menu box

▶ Double-click the Document Control-menu box in the menu bar to close INCOME2.WKS.

If You Want to Quit Works for Now

Application Control-menu box

▶ Double-click the Application Control-menu box in the title bar.

Lesson Summary

To	Do this
Change margins	From the File menu, choose Page Setup, click the Margins tab, type new margin settings, and then press ENTER.
Insert rows or columns	Drag across the row numbers or column labels to highlight as many rows or columns as you want to insert, and then choose Row/Column from the Insert menu.

To	Do this	Button
Change column widths	Drag across the column labels to highlight the columns you want to change, choose Column Width from the Format menu, type the new column width, and then press ENTER.	
Change the number format	Highlight the cells you want to change, choose Number from the Format menu, select a format, type the number of decimals, and then press ENTER.	
Change the alignment of cell entries	Highlight the cells you want to change and then click the Left Align, Center Align, or Right Align button on the toolbar.	
Change the font size of text entries	Highlight the cells you want to change, click the arrow to the right of the Font Size list box on the toolbar, and then select a font size.	
Change the font style of text entries	Highlight the cells you want to change, and then click the Bold, Italic, or Underline button on the toolbar.	
Add borders	Highlight the cells to which you want to add borders, choose Border from the Format menu, select a border, select a line style, and then click the OK button.	
Add shading	Highlight the cells to which you want to add shading, choose Patterns from the Format menu, select a shading pattern from the Pattern list box, and then click the OK button.	
Hide and display gridlines	From the View menu, choose Gridlines.	
Unlock cells	Highlight the cells you want to unlock, choose Protection from the Format menu, turn off the Locked check box, and then click the OK button.	
Turn on cell protection	Choose Protection from the Format menu, turn on the Protect Data check box, and then click the OK button.	
Turn off cell protection	Choose Protection from the Format menu, turn off the Protect Data check box, and then click the OK button.	

To	Do this
Create a header	From the View menu, choose Headers And Footers, type the header text and codes, and then press ENTER.

For more information on	See in the *Microsoft Works User's Guide*
Changing the page setup	Chapter 4, "Changing page and margin settings"
Formatting rows and columns	Chapter 4, "Inserting and deleting rows and columns" Chapter 4, "Changing column width and row height"
Formatting cells	Chapter 4, "Changing number formats" Chapter 4, "Changing alignment in a cell" Chapter 4, "Changing fonts, font sizes, font styles, and colors" Chapter 4, "Adding cell borders" Chapter 4, "Shading cells for emphasis"

For more information on	See in the *Microsoft Works User's Guide*
Using cell protection	Chapter 4, "Protecting entries from changes or deletions"

For online information about	From the Help menu, choose Contents and then
Changing the page setup	Choose "Spreadsheet," choose "Printing a spreadsheet," and select the topic "Setting page size, margins, and orientation."
Formatting rows and columns	Choose "Spreadsheet," choose "Changing the appearance of your spreadsheet," and select "Inserting rows or columns," "Adjusting spreadsheet row height," or "Adjusting spreadsheet column widths."
Formatting cells	Choose "Spreadsheet," choose "Changing the appearance of your spreadsheet," and select "Changing the alignment of a cell," "Changing fonts, font sizes, and font styles in the Spreadsheet," or "Number formats."
Using cell protection	Choose "Spreadsheet," choose "Changing spreadsheet information," and select the topic "Protecting a spreadsheet."

Preview of the Next Lesson

In this lesson, you used a number of formatting features to make your spreadsheets more attractive and enhance their readability. In the next lesson, you'll work with spreadsheet charts, which are visual representations of spreadsheet data. You'll learn the basics of creating and enhancing spreadsheet charts; create bar, line, and pie charts; add chart titles and labels; change the font of chart text; and print charts.

Creating Spreadsheet Charts

Charts are visual representations of spreadsheet data. You use charts to illustrate, analyze, and interpret numerical data and relationships. Because they are visual, charts can often communicate information more quickly than the text and numbers in a spreadsheet.

You need to submit your income analysis for the video department of West Coast Sales to upper management. In addition to your spreadsheet data, you decide to send charts that will quickly illustrate your department's performance. In this lesson, you'll create, enhance, and print spreadsheet charts.

If your screen does not match the illustrations in this lesson, see the Appendix, "Matching the Exercises."

You will learn how to:

- Create bar, line, and pie charts.
- Change from one chart type to another.
- Name and save charts.
- Add titles and labels to a chart.
- Change the font of chart text.
- Preview and print charts.

Estimated lesson time: 20 minutes

Start the lesson

1 In the Startup dialog box, click the Open An Existing Document button.

2 Make sure C:\MSWORKS\WORKSSBS is the current directory.

3 In the File Name list box, double-click 3INCOME.WKS.

   3INCOME.WKS matches the spreadsheet you formatted in Lesson 6.

4 If the document doesn't fill the entire spreadsheet window, click the Maximize button in the spreadsheet window title bar.

Maximize

5 Save the spreadsheet as INCOME3.WKS.

Creating New Charts

For more information about chart types, see the Microsoft Works User's Guide, *Chapter 5, "Changing a chart type."*

You create a chart by highlighting spreadsheet data and letting Works draw the chart for you. You can create as many as eight charts in each spreadsheet, choosing from nine types of charts.

In the next exercises, you'll create a bar chart to illustrate the relationship between the Sales and Income data for the video department.

Create a bar chart

A bar chart shows comparisons of numerical data illustrated with side-by-side or stacked bars.

1 Highlight cells A7 through G7.

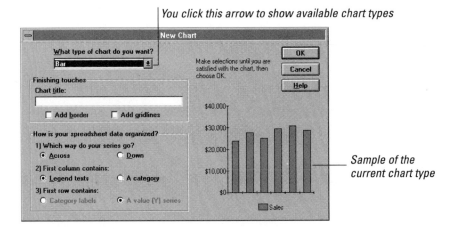

New Chart

2 Click the New Chart button on the toolbar.

The New Chart dialog box appears. The bar chart type is currently selected.

You click this arrow to show available chart types

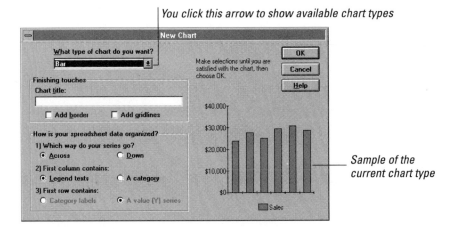

Sample of the current chart type

3 Click the OK button.

Works draws a bar chart based on the highlighted Sales data in the spreadsheet.

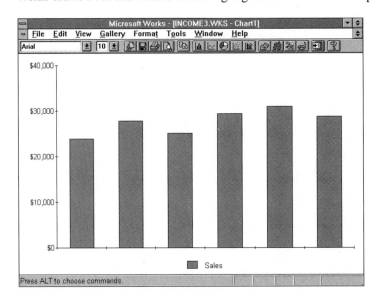

Each bar represents a highlighted Sales value. The set of matching bars is called a *Y-series*. The legend label that appears below the Y-series represents the text in cell A7.

Add a series

The purpose of this bar chart is to show the relationship between two series of values: Sales and Income. Since these values are not adjacent in the spreadsheet, you cannot highlight them together. You must add the second series after Works draws the initial chart.

1 From the Y̲iew menu, choose S̲preadsheet to switch to the spreadsheet window.

2 Highlight cells B13 through G13.

Copy

3 Click the Copy button on the toolbar.

Works copies the Income values to the Clipboard.

4 From the W̲indow menu, choose 2̲ INCOME3.WKS - Chart1 to switch to the chart window.

5 From the E̲dit menu, choose S̲eries.

The Series dialog box appears.

6 Click in the 2nd text box.

7 Click the Paste button in the Series dialog box.

Works pastes the range reference of the values in the Clipboard into the Series dialog box, as shown in the following illustration.

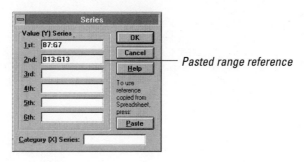

—— Pasted range reference

8 Click the OK button.

Works adds the second series to the chart.

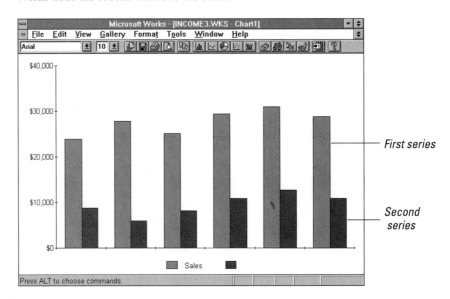

Enhancing Charts

Sometimes, the initial chart that Works draws for you will suit your needs perfectly. Other times, you will want to make some changes and enhancements. For example, your bar chart is currently not very informative because it doesn't contain any identifying titles or labels. In the next exercises, you'll enhance your bar chart by adding titles and labels and changing the font of the chart text.

Add chart titles

1 From the Edit menu, choose Titles.

The Titles dialog box appears. You can specify a title by entering text or typing a cell reference.

2 In the Chart Title text box, type **a1**

The text in cell A1 will appear as the chart title.

3 Press TAB to move to the Subtitle text box, and then type **Video Department**

This text will appear in the chart as a subtitle. The Titles dialog box should now look like the next illustration.

4 Press ENTER.

Your bar chart should now look like the following illustration.

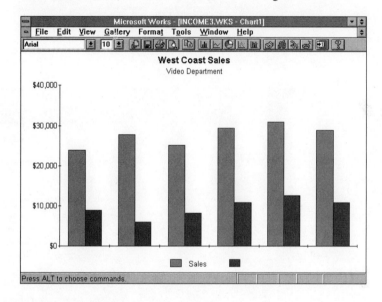

Add category labels

Since your bar chart is meant to show data for the months of January through June, you'll need to add labels to show the month that corresponds to each set of bars. These labels are called *category labels*.

1 From the View menu, choose Spreadsheet.

Copy

2 Highlight cells B5 through G5 and then click the Copy button on the toolbar.

3 From the Window menu, choose 2 INCOME3.WKS - Chart1.

4 From the Edit menu, choose Paste Series.

The Paste Series dialog box appears.

5 Under Use Selection For Series, select Category.

The Paste Series dialog box should now appear as shown in the next illustration.

Select Category

6   Click the OK button.

The category labels appear under each set of bars, as shown in the following illustration.

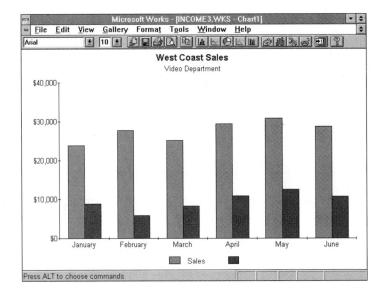

Add a legend label

Your chart currently has a legend label that identifies the Sales series. You need to add another legend label to show that the second series of bars represents Income values.

1   From the Edit menu, choose Legend/Series Labels.

The Legend/Series Labels dialog box appears.

2   Click in the 2nd Value Series text box and then type **a13**

The text in cell A13 will appear as the legend label. The Legend/Series Labels dialog box should now look like the following illustration.

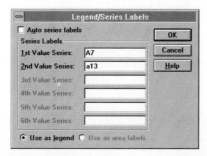

3 Press ENTER to add the legend label to the chart.

Add data labels

Data labels show the spreadsheet values from which each series in a chart is plotted. Adding data labels to your bar chart can eliminate the need to refer to the spreadsheet.

1 From the Edit menu, choose Data Labels.

The Data Labels dialog box appears.

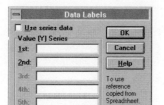

2 Turn on the Use Series Data check box and then click the OK button.

By turning on this check box, you specify the values corresponding to each series as the data labels. The data labels appear above each bar, as shown in the following illustration.

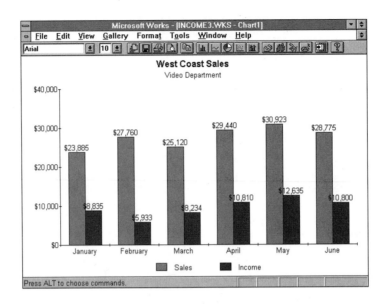

Change the font of chart text

Your bar chart is now more informative than it was originally. You can enhance the information in the chart by changing the font and size of the chart text. You can use two fonts in each chart: one for the chart title and another for all of the other text.

1 Click "West Coast Sales" to highlight the chart title.

Font Size list box

2 Click the arrow to the right of the Font Size list box on the toolbar and then select 14.

Font sizes are measured in *points*. A point is 1/72 inch. The larger the point size you choose, the larger the highlighted text becomes.

3 Click a blank area of the chart to remove the highlighting from the chart title.

4 From the Format menu, choose Font And Style.

The Font And Style For Subtitle And Labels dialog box appears.

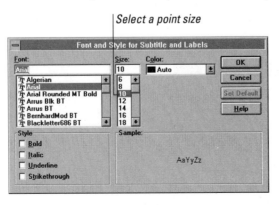

5 In the Size list box, select 8 to indicate 8-point type.

6 Under Style, turn on the Italic check box, and then click the OK button.

The chart labels are now smaller and italicized, as shown in the next illustration.

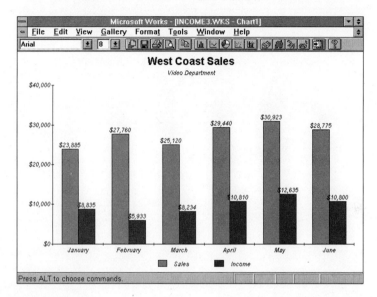

Name the chart

Works automatically names each chart you create Chart1, Chart2, and so on. If you create multiple charts in a spreadsheet, you might want to assign more descriptive names to help you quickly find and switch to a specific chart.

1 From the Tools menu, choose Name Chart.

The Name Chart dialog box appears.

2 Click in the Name text box and then type **Sales/Inc Bar**

The Name Chart dialog box should now match the following illustration.

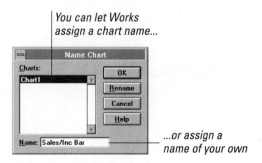

3 Click the Rename button.

The new chart name appears in the Charts list box and also in the title bar of the chart window.

4 Click the OK button.

Save the chart

You save spreadsheets and charts at the same time.

Save

▶ Click the Save button on the toolbar.

The spreadsheet and the chart are saved together.

Creating Additional Charts

You can create as many as eight charts for a single spreadsheet. They can all be the same type of chart or they can be a mixture of various chart types. In the next exercises, you'll create and enhance a line chart using the INCOME3.WKS spreadsheet and then change the chart type.

Create a line chart

A line chart shows changes in numerical data over a period of time. Data is illustrated with one or more lines. You will create a line chart to show fluctuations in Sales and Cost values.

1 From the View menu, choose Spreadsheet to return to the spreadsheet window.

2 Highlight cells A7 through G8.

Since the Sales and Cost values are adjacent in the spreadsheet, you can highlight them together and Works will chart the values simultaneously.

New Chart

3 Click the New Chart button on the toolbar.

4 Click the arrow to the right of the What Type Of Chart Do You Want list box and then select Line.

5 Under Finishing Touches, click in the Chart Title text box.

The text you type in this text box will appear as a title at the top of the chart.

6 Type **Sales vs Cost**

The New Chart dialog box should now look like the following illustration.

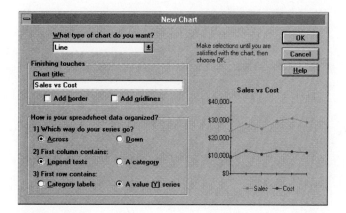

7 Press ENTER.

Works draws a line chart.

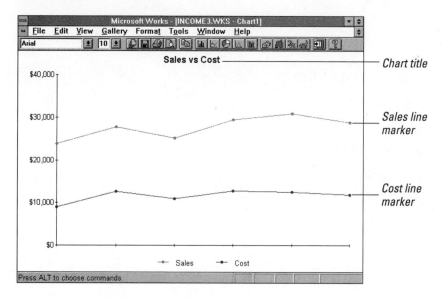

Each line marker represents a Sales or Cost value highlighted in the spreadsheet. Each line is a Y-series.

8 From the Tools menu, choose Name Chart.

9 Click in the Name text box and then type **Sales/Cost Line**

10 Click the Rename button and then click the OK button.

Change the chart type

If you want to view your data in a different way, you don't have to create additional charts; you can simply change the chart type of an existing chart.

3-D Line Chart

1   Click the 3-D Line Chart button on the toolbar.

The 3-D Line dialog box appears.

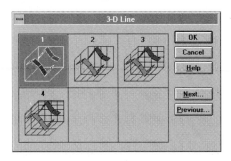

2   Double-click chart option 3.

The chart type changes to a 3-D line chart with gridlines.

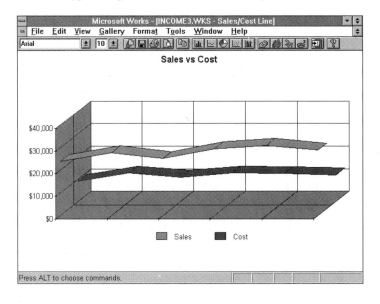

Save

3   Click the Save button on the toolbar to save the charts.

Working with Pie Charts

To make the report you send to management as complete as possible, you decide to show each monthly income value in relation to the total income in your spreadsheet. A pie chart is ideal for this purpose. A pie chart is a circle divided into slices. Each pie slice represents a single value in a Y-series and shows the ratio of each value to the total of the series values. In the next exercises, you'll create a pie chart and add data labels that show each income value.

Create a pie chart

1 From the View menu, choose Spreadsheet.

2 Highlight cells B13 through G13.

Note A pie chart can represent only one series.

New Chart

3 Click the New Chart button on the toolbar.

4 Click the arrow to the right of the What Type Of Chart Do You Want list box and then select Pie.

5 Click in the Chart Title text box and then type **Video Department Income**

6 Press ENTER to create the pie chart shown in the next illustration.

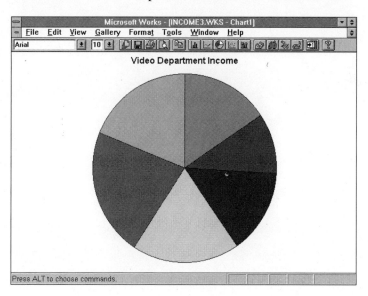

Add data labels

1 From the Edit menu, choose Data Labels.

The Data Labels dialog box appears.

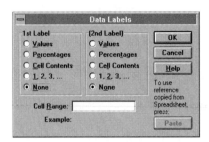

2 Under 1st Label, select Cell Contents.

3 Click in the Cell Range text box and then type **b5:g5**

The entries in cells B5 through G5 (the month labels January through June) will appear as data labels.

4 Under (2nd Label), select Values to indicate that you want each pie slice labeled with its value in relation to the entire pie.

The Data Labels dialog box should now appear as follows.

Select Cell Contents

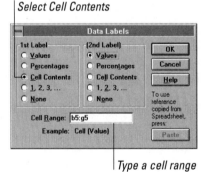

Type a cell range

5 Click the OK button.

The data labels appear next to each pie slice, as shown in the following illustration.

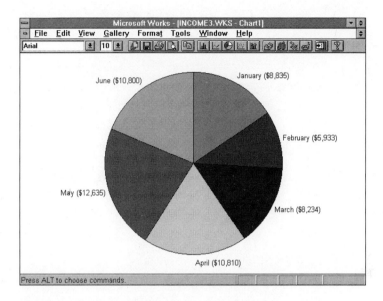

6   From the Tools menu, choose Name Chart.

7   Click in the Name text box and then type **Income Pie**

Save

8   Click the Rename button and then click the OK button.

9   Click the Save button on the toolbar to save your work.

Printing Charts

Your charts are now ready to print. Before you print a chart, you might want to preview it and check to see if you need to make any last minute changes. In the next exercises, you'll preview your bar chart, change the page orientation, and then print the chart.

Preview a chart

1   From the View menu, choose Chart.

The Charts dialog box lists the names of your charts. You must open a chart before you can preview or print it.

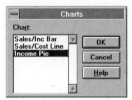

2   Double-click Sales/Inc Bar.

Print Preview

3 Click the Print Preview button on the toolbar.

The bar chart would look better with a horizontal (landscape) page orientation.

4 Click the Cancel button.

Change the page orientation

The page orientation of a chart is not affected by the orientation of the associated spreadsheet. You can set different page orientations for a spreadsheet and its charts.

1 From the File menu, choose Page Setup.

2 Click the Source, Size And Orientation tab if it isn't the displayed tab.

3 Under Orientation, select Landscape, and then click the OK button.

4 Click the Print Preview button on the toolbar to view the new page orientation.

5 Click the Cancel button.

Print a chart

Print

1 Click the Print button on the toolbar.

Works prints the current chart.

Tip If you want to print multiple copies of a chart, choose Print from the File menu and specify the number of copies.

Save

2 When the chart has finished printing, click the Save button on the toolbar to save your work.

One Step Further

After you print your chart, you discover that the bars print in virtually the same shade. You decide to change the colors and fill patterns so you can better differentiate the bars.

Change colors and fill patterns

1 From the Format menu, choose Patterns And Colors.

2 In the Colors list box, select Magenta.

3 Scroll down in the Patterns list box, select Dark //, and then click the Format button.

The color and fill pattern of the first series becomes thick, diagonal magenta stripes.

4 Under Series, select 2nd.

5 Scroll down in the Colors list box and then select Dark Red.

6 Scroll down in the Patterns list box, select Light \\, and click the Format button.

Now the color and fill pattern of the second series changes to thin, diagonal dark red stripes.

7 Click the Close button to close the Patterns And Colors dialog box.

Print

8 Click the Print button on the toolbar to print the chart.

9 Save the spreadsheet and chart.

If You Want to Continue to the Next Lesson

*Document
Control-menu box*

▶ Double-click the Document Control-menu box in the menu bar to close each of the charts and the spreadsheet.

If You Want to Quit Works for Now

*Application
Control-menu box*

▶ Double-click the Application Control-menu box in the title bar.

Lesson Summary

To	Do this	Button
Create a new chart	Highlight the values in the spreadsheet that you want to plot, click the New Chart button on the toolbar, select a chart type, modify the initial chart options, and then click the OK button.	
Add a series	Highlight the series values in the spreadsheet, click the Copy button on the toolbar, switch to the chart window, choose Series from the Edit menu, click in a series text box, click the Paste button, and then click the OK button.	
Name a chart	From the Tools menu, choose Name Chart, select the chart you want to rename, click in the Name text box, type a new name, click the Rename button, and then click the OK button.	
Change the chart type	Click a chart type button on the toolbar, and then double-click a chart option in the dialog box that appears.	
Save charts	Click the Save button on the toolbar.	
Add chart titles	From the Edit menu, choose Titles, type cell references or text in the text boxes, and then press ENTER.	
Add category labels	Highlight the category labels in the spreadsheet, click the Copy button on the toolbar, switch to the chart window, choose Paste Series from the Edit menu, select Category, and then click the OK button.	

To	Do this	Button
Add data labels	From the Edit menu, choose Data Labels, turn on the Use Series Data check box, and then click the OK button.	
Change the font or font size of the chart title	Click the chart title to highlight it, and then select a new font or font size from the toolbar.	Arial ☒ 10 ☒
Change the font or font size of other chart text	Be sure the chart title is not highlighted, and then select a new font or font size from the toolbar.	Arial ☒ 10 ☒
Preview a chart	Click the Print Preview button on the toolbar.	
Change the page orientation	From the File menu, choose Page Setup, click the Source, Size And Orientation tab, select an Orientation option, and then click the OK button.	
Print a chart	Click the Print button on the toolbar.	
Change colors and fill patterns	From the Format menu, choose Patterns And Colors, select a Series option, select a new color and pattern, click the Format button, and then click the OK button.	

For more information on	See in the *Microsoft Works User's Guide*
Creating new charts	Chapter 5, "Creating a chart" Chapter 5, "Adding and deleting chart values" Chapter 5, "Changing a chart type" Chapter 5, "Viewing and naming a chart"
Enhancing charts	Chapter 5, "Adding and deleting chart titles" Chapter 5, "Adding and changing category labels" Chapter 5, "Adding and deleting data labels" Chapter 5, "Changing fonts, font sizes, font styles, and colors" Chapter 5, "Changing colors and patterns"
Printing charts	Chapter 5, "Changing page and margin settings" Chapter 11, "Printing with Works"

For online information about	From the Help menu, choose Contents and then
Creating new charts	Choose "Charting," choose "Charting basics," and select the topic "Creating a chart."
Enhancing charts	Choose "Charting," choose "Changing the appearance of your chart," and select either "Colors, patterns, and markers" or "Changing fonts, font sizes, and font styles in charts."
Printing charts	Choose "Charting" and select the topic "Printing a chart."

Preview of the Next Lesson

In the next lesson, you'll learn how to use templates to quickly create documents with predesigned formats.

Working with Templates

A *template* is a predesigned document with the basic layout, formatting, and sample text already in place. Templates save you time by eliminating the need to create and format documents—you just "fill in the blanks" and print. The templates that are included with Works are called *AutoStart templates*. You use AutoStart templates to quickly create documents such as sales invoices, income statements, and newsletters without performing all of the layout and formatting tasks yourself. In this lesson, you'll use an AutoStart template to produce a sales invoice for one of your customers.

If your screen does not match the illustrations in this lesson, see the Appendix, "Matching the Exercises."

You will learn how to:

- Use AutoStart templates.
- Save a template as a document.
- Save a document as a template.

Estimated lesson time: 15 minutes

Start the lesson

▶ Be sure the Startup dialog box is open.

Open an AutoStart template

1 In the Startup dialog box, click the Use A Template button.

2 Click the arrow to the right of the Choose A Template Group list box.

AutoStart templates provided with Works are organized in three groups: Business, Personal, and Education.

3 Select AutoStart Business.

Within each group, AutoStart templates are organized by category.

4 In the Choose A Category list box, select Billing if it isn't already selected.

Each category contains one or more templates.

5 In the Choose A Template list box, select Sales Invoice if it isn't already selected.

The Startup dialog box should now appear as shown in the following illustration.

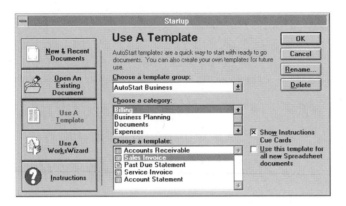

6 Click the OK button.

The Sales Invoice template opens.

Sample text

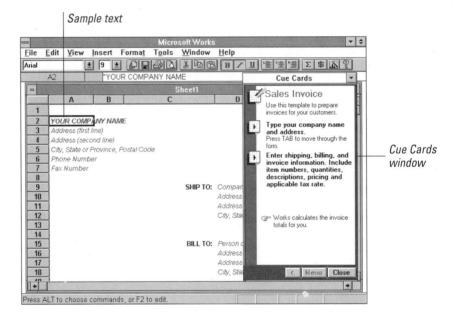

Cue Cards window

The template contains sample text, which you will replace with text of your own. The Cue Cards window automatically appears to provide you with instructions for using the template.

7 Read the instructions in the Cue Cards window.

8 In the Cue Cards window, click the Close button twice to turn off Cue Cards.

You won't be using the Cue Cards for these exercises, but they can be helpful when you're doing your own work.

Note   You can choose Cue Cards from the Help menu to turn on Cue Cards again.

Maximize

9   Click the Maximize button in the document window title bar to make the document fill the entire Works window.

Enter information in the template

Now that you have opened the template, you can enter the information necessary to create your sales invoice. To enter information in a template, you press the TAB key to move the highlight to a sample text entry, and then you type the text that you want to replace it.

1   Type **West Coast Sales** and then press TAB.

The first line of sample text is replaced and the highlight moves to the next line of sample text.

2   Type **Electronics - Music - Videos** and then press TAB.

3   Type **2345 West Mall Circle** and then press TAB.

4   Type **Phoenix, Arizona 85034** and then press TAB.

5   Type **(602) 555-8437** and then press TAB.

6   Press DELETE to remove the last line of sample text and then press TAB.

7   Enter the remaining information in the template, as shown in the following illustration. Press TAB to move between entries. Press SHIFT+TAB to return to a previous entry. Press DELETE to delete any sample text that you do not need.

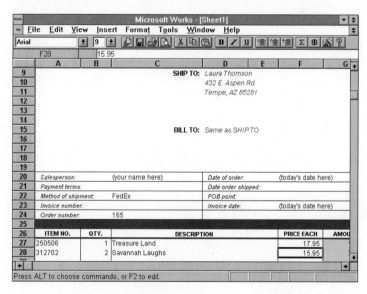

8   Press TAB until the Tax Rate sample text near the bottom of the template is highlighted, and then type **6.8**

9   Press TAB.

Works automatically calculates the extended prices, subtotal, tax due, and total.

Print Preview

10   Click the Print Preview button on the toolbar to preview the invoice.

11   Click the Print button in the Print Preview window to print the invoice.

Save the template as a document

Now that you have created an invoice using the Sales Invoice template, you can save the template as a document and use that document to create additional invoices.

Save

1   Click the Save button on the toolbar.

2   Make C:\MSWORKS\WORKSSBS the current directory if it isn't already.

3   Type **lthomson** and then press ENTER.

The next time you need to generate an invoice for Laura Thomson, you can open LTHOMSON.WKS, make any necessary information changes, and then print the invoice.

4   Close LTHOMSON.WKS.

One Step Further

If the Works AutoStart templates don't quite suit your needs, you can save a document that you've created as a template. You decide to use an existing spreadsheet document to create a template for updating income statements that the department secretary will use. If you don't want the existing data to change, a template which can have only new data entered is ideal.

Save a document as a template

INCOME4.WKS is essentially the same file as completed in Lesson 7, with the exception that an additional column has been added for July, and protection has been turned on for all cells except those in which new data will be entered.

1   Open INCOME4.WKS.

2   Press TAB.

The highlight moves to the first unprotected cell, H7.

3   From the File menu, choose Save As.

4   Click the Template button.

The Save As Template dialog box appears.

5 In the Template Name text box, type **Income Analysis**

6 Click the OK button.

The file is now saved as a template that you can use to create updated income statements.

7 Close INCOME4.WKS.

If You Want to Continue to the Next Lesson

▶ Be sure the Startup dialog box is open.

*Application
Control-menu box*

If You Want to Quit Works for Now

▶ Double-click the Application Control-menu box in the menu bar.

Lesson Summary

To	Do this	Button
Open an AutoStart template	Click the Use A Template button in the Startup dialog box, select a template group, select a template category, and then double-click a template name in the Choose A Template list box.	
Save a template as a document	Click the Save button on the toolbar, type a name for the document in the File Name text box, and then click the OK button.	
Save a document as a template	Open the document and move the highlight to the first unprotected cell. From the File menu, choose Save As, click the Template button, type a template name, and then click the OK button.	

For more information on	See in the *Microsoft Works User's Guide*
Using AutoStart templates	Chapter 2, "Working with the Works AutoStart templates"

For online information about	From the Help menu, choose Contents and then
Working with templates	Choose "Works for Windows Basic Skills," choose "Working with documents," and select the topic "Working with templates."

Preview of the Next Lessons

In Part 3 of this book, you'll learn how to use the Database tool. In Lesson 9, you'll learn the basics of creating a database, editing the information in a database, modifying and formatting a database, and protecting and printing database information. In Lesson 10, you'll learn how to sort, find, replace, and query database information. In Lesson 11, you'll learn how to create, modify, and print database reports.

Review & Practice

In the lessons in Part 2, "Using the Spreadsheet," you learned how to create, edit, format, and print spreadsheets, as well as how to use a number of advanced features to create and work efficiently with complex spreadsheets. You also learned how to create, modify, and print spreadsheet charts and how to use AutoStart templates. If you want to practice these skills and test your understanding before you proceed with the lessons in Part 3, you can work through the Review & Practice section following this lesson.

Part 2   Review & Practice

Before you move on to working with the Database, practice the skills you learned in Part 2 by working through this Review & Practice section. In this section you'll use the Spreadsheet tool to create and save a spreadsheet and chart, enter formulas and functions, edit and format a spreadsheet, protect cell entries, and print a spreadsheet and chart.

Scenario

The Human Resources Administrator for West Coast Sales has recently reported an increase in the number of promotions for retail employees. Your manager, who was very impressed with your report on the video department's first quarter performance, has asked you to analyze the promotion rates in six of the company's primary markets. You decide to use a spreadsheet and a chart for your analysis, which you will later present in a management meeting.

You will review and practice how to:

- Create and save a spreadsheet.
- Use formulas and functions.
- Edit a spreadsheet.
- Format a spreadsheet.
- Protect cells.
- Create a spreadsheet chart.
- Print a spreadsheet and chart.

Estimated practice time: 30 minutes

Step 1: Create and Save a Spreadsheet

In this step, you'll create a spreadsheet, enter text and numbers, and save the spreadsheet.

1   Start the Spreadsheet tool.

2   Enter the text and numbers shown in the following table.

Cell	Entry
A1	Employee Promotion Study
A2	Location
A3	Denver
A4	Phoenix
A5	Boston
A6	New York
A7	Atlanta
A8	San Diego
A9	Totals
B2	Employees
B3	518
B4	600
B5	380
B6	472
B7	835
B8	531
C2	Promotions
C3	82
C4	79
C5	21
C6	33
C7	79
C8	62
D2	Promotion %

3   Save the spreadsheet as PROMOS.WKS in the MSWORKS\WORKSSBS directory.

For more information on	See
Entering text and numbers	Lesson 5
Saving a spreadsheet	Lesson 5

Step 2: Use Formulas and Functions

In this step, you'll enter a formula and a function to begin your analysis.

Enter a formula

▶ In cell D3, enter a formula that calculates the Promotion % value for Denver.

Note   Promotion % is the number of Promotions (C3) divided by the number of Employees (B3).

Enter a function

1   In cell B9, use the SUM function to calculate the total number of employees.

2   Save PROMOS.WKS.

For more information on	See
Entering formulas	Lesson 5
Entering functions	Lesson 5

Step 3: Edit a Spreadsheet

In this step, you'll edit cell entries, copy formulas and a function to complete your spreadsheet data, and find and replace text.

Edit cell entries

1   In cell C5, replace the number 21 with the number 29.

2   Move to cell A1, click the formula bar to turn on EDIT mode, and then change the text entry from "Employee Promotion Study" to "Employee Promotion Analysis."

Copy cell entries

1   Use Fill Down from the Edit menu to copy the formula in cell D3 to cells D4 through D9.

2   Use drag-and-drop to copy the function in cell B9 to cell C9.

3   Save PROMOS.WKS.

Find and replace text

▶ Use the Replace dialog box to replace "Location" with "City."

For more information on	See
Editing cell entries	Lesson 5
Copying cell entries	Lesson 5
Finding and replacing text	Lesson 5

Step 4: Format a Spreadsheet

In this step, you'll make your promotion analysis spreadsheet easy to read by changing column widths; inserting rows; changing number formats and the alignment, font, size, and style of text entries; and adding borders.

Change column widths

1   Highlight columns A through D.

2   Change the width of the highlighted columns to 12.

Insert rows

1   Highlight row 2 and then insert one row.

2   Highlight row 10 and then insert one row.

Change number formats

1   Highlight cells B4 through C11.

2   Open the Number dialog box and then apply the Comma format with no decimals.

3   Highlight cells D4 through D11 and apply the Percent format with one decimal.

Change the alignment of text entries

1   Right-align the entries in cells B3 through D3.

2   Highlight cells A1 through D1.

3   Open the Alignment dialog box and then center the entry across the current selection.

Change the font, size, and style of text entries

1   Highlight cells A1 through D11.

2   Change the font to Times New Roman.

3   Highlight cell A1 and then change the font size to 12.

4   Highlight cells A3 through D3 and then change the font style to Bold.

Add borders

1 Highlight cells B9 through D9.

2 Open the Border dialog box and then apply the second line style as a bottom border.

3 Highlight cells B11 through D11.

4 Open the Border dialog box and then apply the double line style as a bottom border.

5 Highlight cells A3 through D3.

6 Open the Border dialog box and then apply the second line style as an outline border.

7 Save PROMOS.WKS.

For more information on	See
Changing column widths	Lesson 6
Inserting rows	Lesson 6
Changing number formats	Lesson 6
Changing the alignment of text entries	Lesson 6
Changing the font, size, and style of text entries	Lesson 6
Adding borders	Lesson 6

Step 5: Protect Cells

In this step, you'll use cell protection to prevent unauthorized or accidental changes to your spreadsheet.

Unlock cells

1 Highlight cells B4 through C9.

2 Open the Protection dialog box and then unlock the highlighted cells.

Turn on cell protection

1 Open the Protection dialog box and then turn on cell protection.

2 Press CTRL+HOME to move the highlight to cell A1.

Your spreadsheet should now match the following illustration.

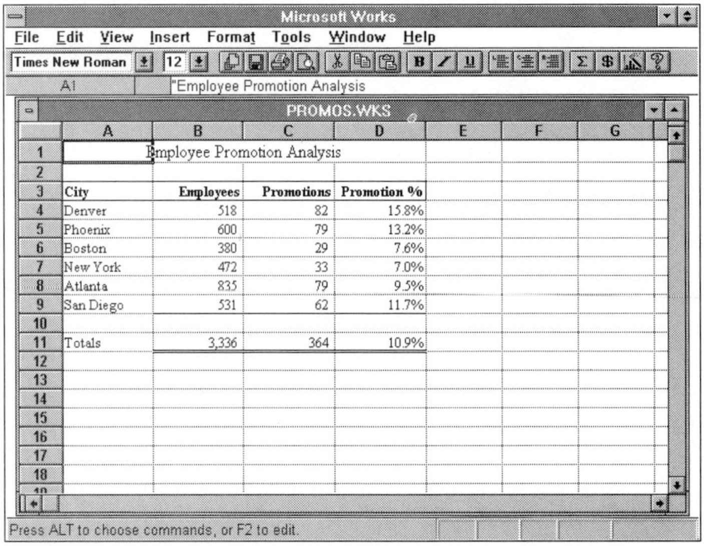

3 Save PROMOS.WKS.

For more information on	See
Unlocking cells	Lesson 6
Using cell protection	Lesson 6

Step 6: Create a Spreadsheet Chart

In this step, you'll create a bar chart based on your spreadsheet, add a title to the chart, change the font of chart text, and name and save the chart.

Create a bar chart

1 Highlight cells A3 through C9 and then open the New Chart dialog box.

2 Specify the chart title "Employee Promotion Analysis."

3 Create the chart.

Add a chart title

1 Open the Titles dialog box.

2 Add the subtitle "Promotions by City."

Change the font of chart text

1 Highlight the chart title.

2 Change the font to Times New Roman and the font size to 14.

3 Remove the highlighting from the chart title.

4 Change the font of the other chart text to Times New Roman.

Name and save the chart

1 Open the Name Chart dialog box.

2 Name the chart "Promos."

3 Save PROMOS.WKS.

Your completed chart should look like the following illustration.

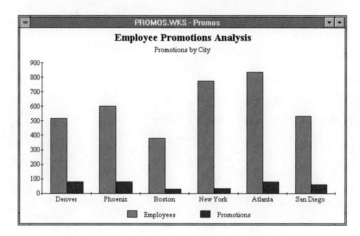

For more information on	See
Creating and modifying charts	Lesson 7

Step 7: Print a Spreadsheet and Chart

In this step, you'll change the page orientation, change margins, and preview and print your spreadsheet and chart.

Change the page orientation

1 Open the Page Setup dialog box.

2 Display the Source, Size And Orientation options.

3 Change the Orientation setting to Landscape.

4 Switch to the spreadsheet.

5 Change the page orientation of the spreadsheet to Landscape.

Change margins

1 Open the Page Setup dialog box.

2 Display the Margins options.

3 Change the top margin to 2.5 inches and the left margin to 3 inches.

Preview and print a spreadsheet and chart

1 Click the Print Preview button on the toolbar.

2 Click the Print button in the Print Preview window to print the spreadsheet.

3 Switch to the Promos chart.

4 Click the Print Preview button on the toolbar.

5 Click the Print button in the Print Preview window to print the chart.

6 Click the Save button on the toolbar to save your work.

For more information on	See
Changing the page orientation	Lesson 6
Changing margins	Lesson 6
Previewing and printing a spreadsheet	Lesson 5
Previewing and printing a chart	Lesson 7

If You Want to Continue to the Next Lesson

1 Switch to the spreadsheet.

2 Double-click the Document Control-menu box in the spreadsheet window title bar.

If You Want to Quit Works for Now

▶ Double-click the Application Control-menu box in the Microsoft Works title bar.

Getting Started with the Database

The Database is a tool you can use to create electronic filing systems and organize information such as a mailing list of your clients, a list of your favorite books, or a product inventory. You can use and view data stored in a database in different ways. For example, you can sort the information alphabetically or numerically, select a specific group of customers and print mailing labels, view the information one item at a time, or view all of the information at the same time.

At West Coast Sales, all department managers use the Database tool to keep track of the product inventory for their individual departments. In the video department, your database stores information such as the stock number, title, star, distributor, year issued, quantity, and price of each video you carry. You are responsible for keeping the database information current and providing information and reports to management. In this lesson, you'll learn the basics of creating, editing, and formatting a database and printing database information.

If your screen does not match the illustrations in this lesson, see the Appendix, "Matching the Exercises."

You will learn how to:

- Open a database.
- Insert fields and add labels.
- Enter and edit records and field entries.
- Format database fields and forms.
- Print database records.

Estimated lesson time: 30 minutes

Start the lesson

▶ Be sure the Startup dialog box is open.

Creating a Database

A *database* is an organized collection of information. With an electronic database, you can store large amounts of related information and then view and print the information in many different ways. A database contains the components described in the following table.

Component	Description
Records	Collections of related information about a person, place, item, or event. For example, in a database that stores names and addresses, the name and address of one person is a record.
Fields	Categories of information. For example, in a database that stores names and addresses, "First Name" might be one field, "Last Name" another field, and "City," "State," and "Zip Code" other fields. All the fields for one person or item make up a record.

You create a database by opening a new database window, inserting fields and adding labels on a *database form*, and saving the database. A database form is essentially a data entry form that you can use to enter information into a database. In the next exercises, you'll open the database that contains your video inventory, and add new information to it.

Open an existing database

When you installed the practice files in the "Getting Ready" section, the files were copied to your hard disk and stored in the C:\MSWORKS\WORKSSBS directory. To locate and access the files, you must make the directory in which they are stored the current directory.

1   Click the Open An Existing Document button in the Startup dialog box.

The Open dialog box appears.

For information about creating a new database, see the Microsoft Works User's Guide, *Chapter 6, "Beginning a database."*

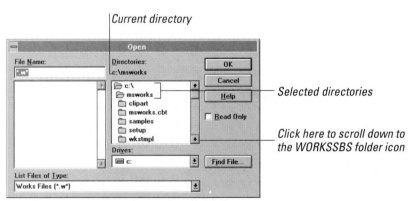

To make C:\MSWORKS\WORKSSBS the current directory, you must select each of the component directories (C:\, MSWORKS, and WORKSSBS). To select a directory, you double-click the corresponding folder icon. When a directory is selected, its icon appears as an open folder.

Note   If the C:\ and MSWORKS folder icons are already open, C:\MSWORKS is the current directory. If this is the case, you can skip to step 3.

---

2   In the Directories list box, double-click the C:\ folder icon and then double-click the MSWORKS folder icon to make C:\MSWORKS the current directory.

3   Scroll down in the Directories list box and then double-click the WORKSSBS folder icon to open the directory in which the practice files are stored.

Now that you have selected the WORKSSBS directory, a list of available files appears in the File Name list box, as shown in the following illustration.

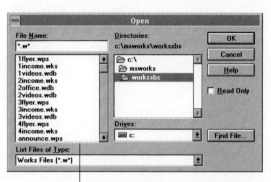

│ *A list of available files appears here*

4   In the File Name list box, double-click 1VIDEOS.WDB to open the file.

The file opens in *form view.* In form view, database records appear on a database form and can be viewed only one at a time.

Maximize

5   Click the Maximize button in the 1VIDEOS.WDB title bar to make the database fill the entire window.

Your video database contains eight fields identified by *field names* (Stock #:, Title:, Star:, and so on) and 48 records. The record number indicator in the bottom left corner of the database window shows you the number of the current record. Your screen should look like the following illustration.

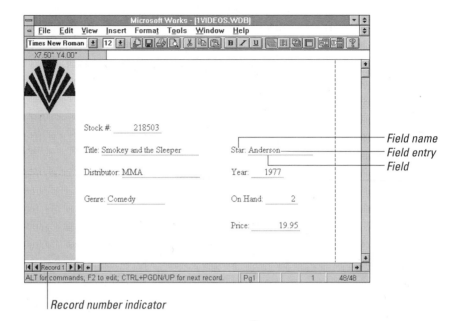

Field name
Field entry
Field

Record number indicator

Insert a field

Although your database already contains important information, you feel that it would be a good idea to show the inventory value for each video (the amount of money made if all available copies of the video are sold). Before you can show this information, you need to insert a field for it in the database form.

Notice the X and Y coordinates in the left side of the formula bar. You can use these coordinates to position the insertion point before inserting the field. That way, you can line the fields up with each other by matching their X or Y coordinates.

1   Click in the blank area to the left of the Price: field name and below the Genre: field name.

2   Using the arrow keys, position the insertion point at X2.42" Y4.00".

The coordinate X2.42" matches the position of the Stock #, Title, Distributor, and Genre column. The coordinate Y4.00" matches the position of the Price row.

3   Type **Inventory Value:**

Field names can contain as many as 15 characters. In form view, field names must be followed by a colon (:). If you don't type a colon, the field will not be created.

Your database form should now look like the following.

X and Y coordinates

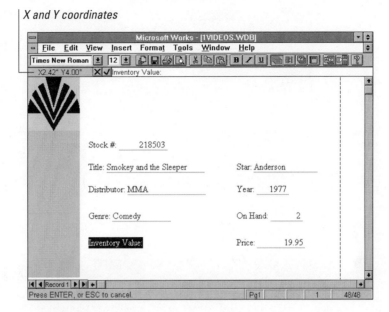

4 Press ENTER.

The Field Size dialog box appears.

If the field size that you use when you create a field is not appropriate for the information you enter into the field, you can change it. See "Change the size of fields" later in this lesson.

The field size determines how much of the contents of a field will appear on screen.

5 Press ENTER to insert the new field with the column width Works suggests.

Your database form should now match the following illustration.

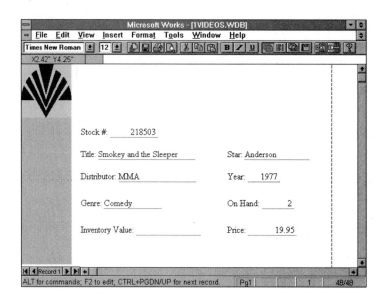

You will enter information in the Inventory Value field later in this lesson.

Add a label

Labels are titles or other descriptive text on a database form. They are not the same as field names, which identify the types of information in fields. You decide to add a label at the top of your form to give the form a title.

1 Click the center of the blank area at the top of the form.

2 Type **Video Inventory** and then press ENTER.

Tip   If you would like to end a label with a colon, type a quotation mark (") before you type the colon so that Works doesn't create a new field.

Move the label

After you create a label, you can move it to a new position on the database form.

1 Position the pointer on the highlighted label.

The pointer changes to the DRAG pointer.

2 Hold down the mouse button, drag the label to the coordinates X2.42" Y1.42", and then release the mouse button.

Note   You can move a field or field name in the same way that you move a label.

Your database form should now look like the following illustration.

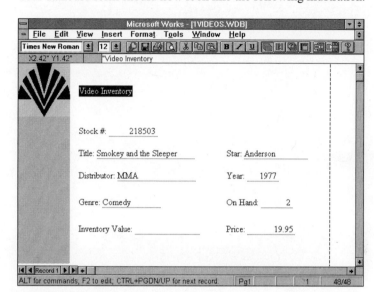

Save the database

As you create or change a database, your work is held in the computer's temporary memory. To ensure that you don't lose data, you should save your database periodically.

1 From File menu, choose Save As.

The Save As dialog box appears.

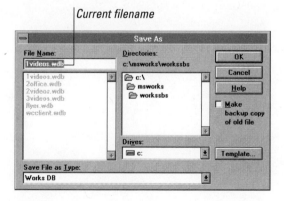

Current filename

2 Type **videos1** in the File Name text box and then click the OK button.

The database is saved with the name VIDEOS1.WDB. The current name of the database appears in the database window title bar.

Editing Database Information

You will need to edit a database for a variety of reasons: You might make mistakes while entering data, or perhaps you buy a new product and need to add it to your inventory, or you discontinue a product and need to delete it from your inventory. In the next exercises, you'll edit your database to reflect changes in your video inventory.

Enter records

You have purchased two new videos and need to add their inventory information to your database. You'll enter one record in form view and the other record in *list view*. Unlike form view, which shows you one record at a time, list view allows you to see several records at once. Although you can perform many actions in a database in either view, you might find it easier to use form view when working with one record at a time and use list view when working with and comparing several records at a time.

Last Record

1   In the bottom left corner of the database window, click the Last Record button to display a blank record.

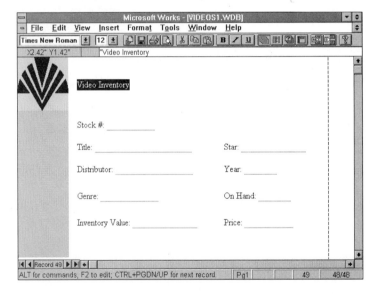

2   Click the line to the right of the Stock #: field name to highlight the field as shown in the following illustration.

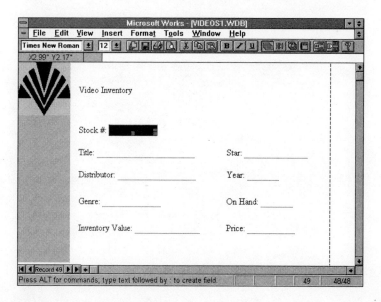

Note   The gray boxes that appear in the highlighted field are *sizing handles*, which you can drag to change the size of the field.

3   Type **101507** and then press TAB.

The first field entry is entered and the highlight moves to the Title field. The field entry you just entered is the stock number for the new record. Since every video in your inventory has a different stock number, the entries you make in the Stock # field must be unique for each record in the database.

4   Type **American You** and then press TAB to move to the Star field.

Note   Pressing TAB highlights the next field; pressing SHIFT+TAB highlights the previous field.

5   Type the other field entries shown below, pressing TAB after each entry.

Field	Entry
Star	**Schneider**
Distributor	**MOM**
Year	**1992**
Genre	**Drama**
On Hand	**2**
Inventory Value	(Press TAB to leave this blank for now)
Price	**34.95**

When you press TAB after the last field entry, the new record is saved, and a blank record displays so you can add information for another new record if you want to. You will enter the next new record in list view instead.

List View

6 Click the List View button on the toolbar to switch to list view.

Your screen should look like the following illustration.

	Stock #	Title	Star	Distributor	Year	Genre	Price	On Hand	In
1	218503	Smokey and the Sle	Anderson	MMA	1977	Comedy	19.95	2	
2	691006	People in the Basen	Langer	Universe	1991	Horror	29.99	3	
3	390005	Sounding Like Musi	Anderson	Wolf	1975	Music	27.95	4	
4	976407	Defending Your Life	Brookman	Wilson	1991	Comedy	19.49	3	
5	250506	Treasure Land	Foster	MOM	1973	Family	17.95	1	
6	151704	Red Thunder	Schneider	United	1982	Action	14.95	2	
7	101277	High Afternoon	Duke	Capricorn	1952	Drama	18.95	2	
8	495408	Hamburger Mountain	James	Wilson	1987	Action	14.95	2	
9	321000	Screamers	Lock	Wolf	1988	Horror	19.95	3	
10	913400	Little Match Boy	Pulliam	Universe	1987	Family	21.95	2	
11	528604	Night of Mischief	Gertzer	Wolf	1985	Comedy	19.95	1	
12	263806	Strike Up the Band	Garling	MOM	1940	Music	16.99	1	
13	202101	An Officer, Not A Ge	Gore	Nielson	1982	Drama	15.95	2	
14	104000	Frankenstein Two	Curtis	Wolf	1990	Horror	29.95	2	
15	525005	East Side Story	Woodington	MOM	1961	Music	18.95	1	
16	734905	War of the Wizards	Curtis	Neilson	1986	Sci-Fi	28.95	3	
17	630301	Missing	Hartman	MMA	1984	Drama	19.95	2	
18	312702	Savannah Laughs	Scott	Wolf	1982	Family	15.95	2	
19	726604	Young Gunners	Phillips	United	1988	Action	14.95	3	
20	960906	Witches World	Phillips	Wilson	1989	Family	19.95	2	

— *Field names*

Record numbers

In list view, the database records appear in table format, similar to a spreadsheet. You can use this view to look at or compare several records at once. Changes you make in list view are reflected in form view. Likewise, changes you make in form view are reflected in list view. For example, record 49, which you added in form view, appears in list view.

7 Scroll down and then click record number 50 to highlight the entire record, as shown in the following illustration.

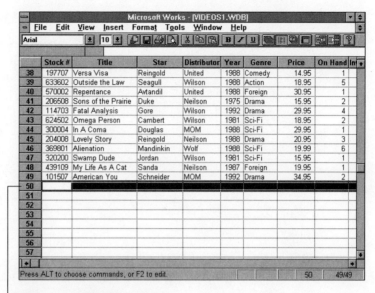

Click here to highlight the record

8 Type the following field entries, pressing ENTER after each entry.

Field	Entry
Stock #	**439901**
Title	**Sabrina**
Star	**Boghart**
Distributor	**Neilson**
Year	**1954**
Genre	**Comedy**
Price	**13.95**
On Hand	**1**
Inventory Value	(Press ENTER to leave this blank for now)

Enter a formula

So far, you haven't made any entries for the Inventory Value field because inventory value was set up to be the result of a calculation. You can use a *formula* to calculate the inventory value of each video.

A formula is a field entry that uses the contents of other fields to make a calculation. All formulas begin with an equal sign (=) and can contain field names, mathematical operators (+, -, *, or /), and numbers.

1 Click the Inventory Value field for record number 50, as shown in the following illustration.

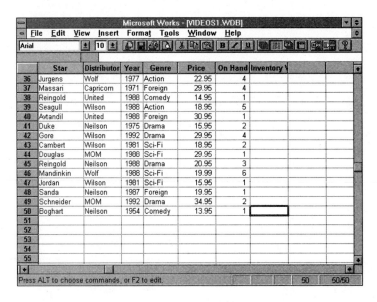

2 Type **=price*on hand**

This formula will calculate the inventory value by multiplying the value in the Price field by the value in the On Hand field.

Your screen should now match the following illustration.

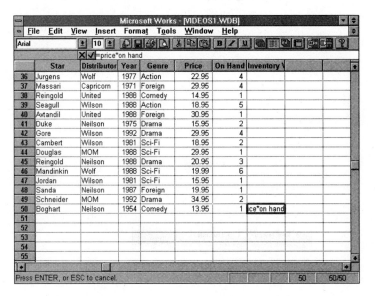

3 Press ENTER.

The formula calculates an inventory value for every record in the database, as shown in the next illustration.

	Star	Distributor	Year	Genre	Price	On Hand	Inventory V
36	Jurgens	Wolf	1977	Action	22.95	4	91.8
37	Massari	Capricorn	1971	Foreign	29.95	4	119.8
38	Reingold	United	1988	Comedy	14.95	1	14.95
39	Seagull	Wilson	1988	Action	18.95	5	94.75
40	Avtandil	United	1988	Foreign	30.95	1	30.95
41	Duke	Neilson	1975	Drama	15.95	2	31.9
42	Gore	Wilson	1992	Drama	29.95	4	119.8
43	Cambert	Wilson	1981	Sci-Fi	18.95	2	37.9
44	Douglas	MOM	1988	Sci-Fi	29.95	1	29.95
45	Reingold	Neilson	1988	Drama	20.95	3	62.85
46	Mandinkin	Wolf	1988	Sci-Fi	19.99	6	119.94
47	Jordan	Wilson	1981	Sci-Fi	15.95	1	15.95
48	Sanda	Neilson	1987	Foreign	19.95	1	19.95
49	Schneider	MOM	1992	Drama	34.95	2	69.9
50	Boghart	Neilson	1954	Comedy	13.95	1	13.95

Note   You can also enter a formula in form view.

Replace a field entry

As your inventory fluctuates, you replace field entries to reflect the changes. For example, you reordered two copies of a video and, now that they have arrived, you need to update the On Hand field for the corresponding record. You can quickly go to the record by searching for a specific title.

1 From the Edit menu, choose Find.

The Find dialog box appears.

2 Type **East Side Story** in the Find What text box.

This specifies the title you want to find.

3 In the Match section, select All Records.

This specifies that Works should search all records for the text you typed in the Find What text box. The Find dialog box should look like the following.

Select All Records

4 Click the OK button.

Only record 15 appears in the database window and the Find dialog box closes.

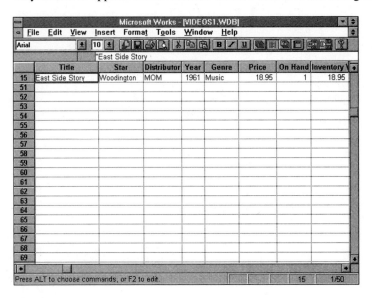

5 Highlight the On Hand field.

6 Type **3** and then press ENTER to replace the field entry.

Notice that the Inventory Value field automatically recalculates.

Edit a field entry

It has come to your attention that you have entered an incorrect price for one of the videos. However, you need to change only one digit in the price, so you choose to use the EDIT feature instead of replacing the entire entry.

1 From the Edit menu, choose Find.

2 Type **Murmur of the Heart** In the Find What text box.

3   In the Match section, select All Records, and then click the OK button.

Only record 37 appears in the database window.

4   Highlight the Price field.

5   Click in the formula bar to the right of the price.

Clicking the formula bar turns on EDIT mode. An insertion point and the contents of the field now appear in the formula bar.

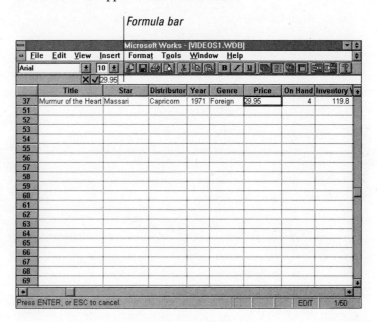

Formula bar

6   Press the LEFT ARROW key three times.

The insertion point moves left three characters in the formula bar.

7   Press BACKSPACE to delete the character to the left of the insertion point.

Note   You can press DELETE to delete the character to the right of the insertion point.

---

8   Type **7** and then press ENTER.

The edited entry now appears in the Price field, as shown in the next illustration.

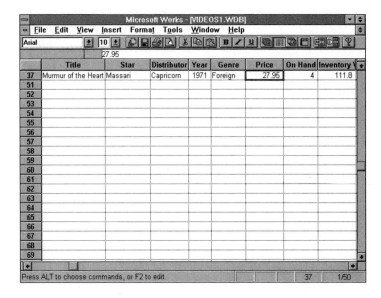

Delete a record

You decide to stop selling one of the less popular videos in your inventory, so you must delete the record from your database. The easiest way to delete a record in list view is to select the entire record and then delete it.

1　From the View menu, choose Show All Records.

　　All the records now display in the database window.

2　Scroll up through your database and then click record number 24 to highlight the entire record, as shown in the following illustration.

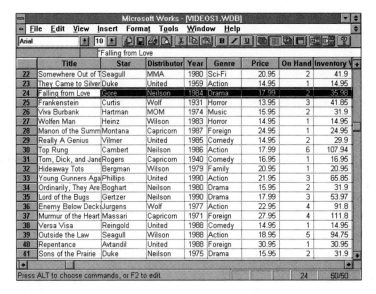

3 From the Insert menu, choose Delete Record/Field.

The record is deleted and all subsequent records are renumbered.

Tip   You can also delete a record in form view by displaying the record you want to delete and then choosing Delete Record from the Insert menu.

Undo a change

You realize that you shouldn't delete the information until the existing inventory is sold. You can use the Undo feature to get the record back.

Note   The Undo feature will reverse only the *last* action performed.

---

1 From the Edit menu, choose Undo Delete Record.

The Undo command reverses the last action and restores the deleted record.

Note   You can undo most of the editing and formatting changes you make; however, you cannot undo actions such as saving a document.

Save

2 Click the Save button on the toolbar to save your work.

Formatting a Database

You can use a variety of formatting features to improve the appearance of your database and make the field entries easier to read and interpret. In the next exercises, you'll change the size of several fields so that data appears properly on the screen and in print, and you'll change the number format of the Price and Inventory Value fields so that the field entries appear as dollar amounts. You'll also use different alignments and fonts and add borders and shading to improve the appearance of your database form.

Change the size of fields

You change the size of a field when you want to display or print more or less of the field's data or change the amount of space between columns of data. The size of a field does not affect the amount of data you can store in the field, but only the amount of data that appears on the screen and in print.

1 Click the Inventory Value field for record number 24.

Currently, you can't see the entire field name for the Inventory Value field because the field is too small. You can show the entire field name by increasing the size of the field.

2   From the Format menu, choose Field Width.

The Field Width dialog box appears.

3   Type **15** in the Width text box and then press ENTER.

The field width changes from 10 characters to 15 characters.

4   Scroll to view the entire Inventory Value field.

Tip   You can also drag a field name border to change the width of a field.

---

5   Move the highlight to the Title field of record 1.

The field width is too small to display all of the entries in their entirety.

6   Double-click the Title field name, as shown in the following.

Double-click here to assign the best fit

	Stock #	Title	Star	Distributor	Year	Genre	Price	On Hand	In
1	218503	Smokey and the Sle	Anderson	MMA	1977	Comedy	19.95	2	
2	691006	People in the Basen	Langer	Universe	1991	Horror	29.99	3	
3	390005	Sounding Like Music	Anderson	Wolf	1975	Music	27.95	4	
4	976407	Defending Your Life	Brookman	Wilson	1991	Comedy	19.49	3	
5	250506	Treasure Land	Foster	MOM	1973	Family	17.95	1	
6	151704	Red Thunder	Schneider	United	1982	Action	14.95	2	
7	101277	High Afternoon	Duke	Capricorn	1952	Drama	18.95	2	
8	495408	Hamburger Mountair	James	Wilson	1987	Action	14.95	2	
9	321000	Screamers	Lock	Wolf	1988	Horror	19.95	3	
10	913400	Little Match Boy	Pulliam	Universe	1987	Family	21.95	2	
11	528604	Night of Mischief	Gertzer	Wolf	1985	Comedy	19.95	1	

Works automatically adjusts the field size to accommodate the width of the longest entry. This feature is called the *best fit*. Your screen should now look like the following illustration.

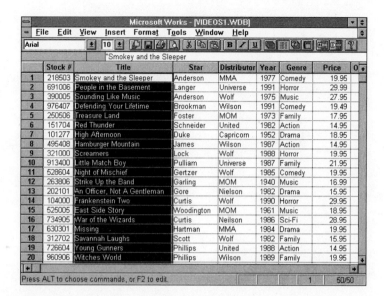

7   Click in the Inventory Value field for record number 1.

Form View

8   Click the Form View button on the toolbar to switch to form view.

Although you changed the size of the Inventory Value field in list view, the field size did *not* change in form view. You will change the size of the Inventory Value field to reduce the space between the field name and the field data.

9   From the Format menu, choose Field Size.

The Field Size dialog box appears.

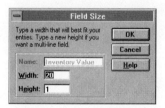

10   Type **15** in the Width text box and then press ENTER.

The field width changes to 15 characters and the field data is now closer to the field name.

Tip   You can also drag a sizing handle, which is one of the small squares that appear on the bottom and right borders of a highlighted field, to change the size of a field in form view.

Change number formats

1 Make sure the Inventory Value field is highlighted, hold down CTRL, and then click the Price field.

Both the Inventory Value and Price fields should now be highlighted, as shown in the following illustration.

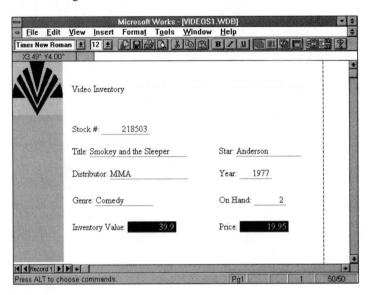

2 From the Format menu, choose Number.

The Number dialog box appears.

3 Under Format, select Currency.

The Number dialog box should now match the following illustration.

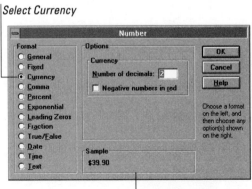

Select Currency

Sample of chosen format

The Currency format displays numbers with a leading dollar sign, thousands separators, and a specified number of decimals.

4 Click the OK button to apply the new number format.

The Inventory Value and Price field entries for every record now appear in the Currency format with two decimals. Your screen should look like the following.

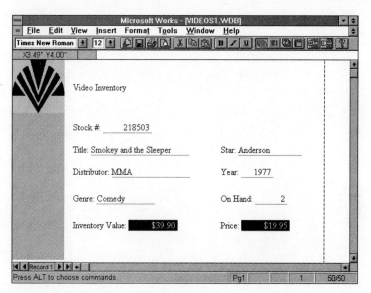

Change the alignment of field entries

So far, you've made your database easier to read by changing field sizes and number formats. Now you will make the Inventory Value and Price fields stand out a bit by changing the alignment of the data in these fields.

1 Make sure the Inventory Value and Price fields are still highlighted. If they aren't, click the Inventory Value field, hold down CTRL, and then click the Price field.

2 From the Format menu, choose Alignment.

The Alignment dialog box appears.

3 Under Alignment, select Center.

The Alignment dialog box should now appear as follows.

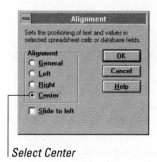

Select Center

4 Click the OK button.

The entries are centered within the borders of each field. Changing the alignment of a field in form view or list view also changes the alignment in the other view.

Change the font, size, and style of text

Your database form currently contains all the information you need, but it's difficult to distinguish some of the fields from their field names because all of the text looks the same. You can solve this problem and add visual appeal to your form by changing the font, size, and style of the text.

1 Position the pointer above and to the left of the label "Video Inventory."

2 Drag the pointer to the bottom right corner of the database window.

A dotted border appears as you drag the pointer.

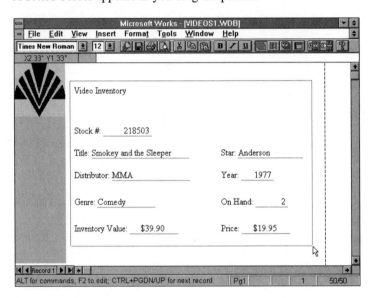

3 Release the mouse button.

All of the enclosed objects are now highlighted.

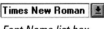

Font Name list box

4 Click the arrow to the right of the Font Name list box on the toolbar and then select Arial.

The font of the highlighted text changes from Times New Roman to Arial.

Bold

5 Click the Bold button on the toolbar.

The highlighted text is now bold.

6 Click a blank area on the form to remove the highlighting.

7 Hold down CTRL and then click each of the fields to highlight all of them.

Only the fields are highlighted; the field names and the Video Inventory label should not be highlighted. Your screen should match the following illustration.

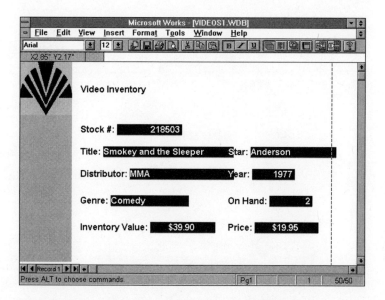

Font Size list box

8 Click the arrow to the right of the Font Size list box on the toolbar and select 10.

The font size of the field entries changes from 12 to 10.

9 Click the Bold button on the toolbar to turn off bold for the field entries.

10 Highlight the label "Video Inventory," click the arrow to the right of the Font Size list box, and then select 24.

11 Click the Italic button on the toolbar to italicize the label.

Italic

Every record in the database will reflect your changes. Your database form should look like the following illustration.

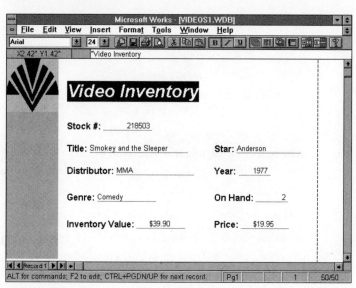

Add borders

Due to constant inquiries about video prices, you decide to make the price field stand out from the rest of your database form so you can quickly look up a price at a glance. You can draw attention to the field by adding a border.

1 Highlight the Price field.

2 From the Format menu, choose Border.

The Border dialog box appears.

3 Under Line Style, click the third line style from the top to select it.

The Border dialog box should now match the next illustration.

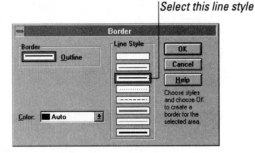

Select this line style

4 Click the OK button to add the border.

5 Click a blank area of the form so you can see the border.

Add shading

1 Highlight the label "Video Inventory."

2 From the Format menu, choose Patterns.

The Patterns dialog box appears.

3 Under Shading, click the arrow to the right of the Pattern list box.

4 Select the seventh shading pattern from the top (the horizontal line pattern).

You will have to scroll down in the Pattern list box to see the seventh pattern. The Patterns dialog box should now look like the following.

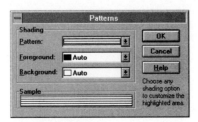

5 Click the OK button to add the shading to the label.

6   Click a blank area on the form to remove the highlighting.

Your database form should now match the following illustration.

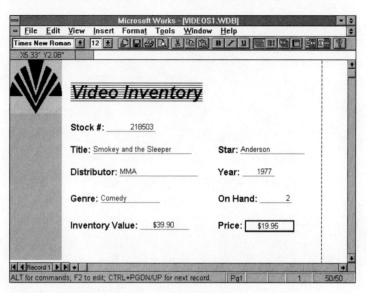

Save

7   Click the Save button on the toolbar to save your work.

Printing Database Records

You can print your database records in form view or in list view. In form view, you normally print one record at a time, and in list view you print multiple records in table format. You can selectively print records by hiding certain records and then printing either the hidden or the displayed records. You can also add informative headers and footers, use Page Setup commands to change the page orientation and printing options, and preview the records before you print.

In the next exercises, you'll prepare and print a list of several of your best selling videos and you'll add a header and a footer to enhance the appearance and clarity of the list. Your list will contain only 9 of the 50 records in the database. You can easily specify that only those 9 records print.

Select records for printing

List View

1   Click the List View button to switch to list view.

2   Drag across record numbers 1 through 4 to highlight the records, as shown in the following illustration.

Drag across these record numbers to highlight the rows

	Stock #	Title	Star	Distributor	Year	Genre	Price	O
1	218503	Smokey and the Sleeper	Anderson	MMA	1977	Comedy	$19.95	
2	691006	People in the Basement	Langer	Universe	1991	Horror	$29.99	
3	390005	Sounding Like Music	Anderson	Wolf	1975	Music	$27.95	
4	976407	Defending Your Lifetime	Brookman	Wilson	1991	Comedy	$19.49	
5	250506	Treasure Land	Foster	MOM	1973	Family	$17.95	
6	151704	Red Thunder	Schneider	United	1982	Action	$14.95	
7	101277	High Afternoon	Duke	Capricorn	1952	Drama	$18.95	
8	495408	Hamburger Mountain	James	Wilson	1987	Action	$14.95	
9	321000	Screamers	Lock	Wolf	1988	Horror	$19.95	
10	913400	Little Match Boy	Pulliam	Universe	1987	Family	$21.95	
11	528604	Night of Mischief	Gertzer	Wolf	1985	Comedy	$19.95	
12	263806	Strike Up the Band	Garling	MOM	1940	Music	$16.99	
13	202101	An Officer, Not A Gentleman	Gore	Nielson	1982	Drama	$15.95	
14	104000	Frankenstein Two	Curtis	Wolf	1990	Horror	$29.95	
15	525005	East Side Story	Woodington	MOM	1961	Music	$18.95	
16	734905	War of the Wizards	Curtis	Neilson	1986	Sci-Fi	$28.95	
17	630301	Missing	Hartman	MMA	1984	Drama	$19.95	
18	312702	Savannah Laughs	Scott	Wolf	1982	Family	$15.95	
19	726604	Young Gunners	Phillips	United	1988	Action	$14.95	
20	960906	Witches World	Phillips	Wilson	1989	Family	$19.95	

Press ALT to choose commands, or F2 to edit.

3 From the Vi̲ew menu, choose Hi̲de Record.

Records 1 through 4 are now hidden and are not available for printing.

4 Highlight records 33 through 37.

5 From the Vi̲ew menu, choose Hi̲de Record.

Records 33 through 37 are now hidden and are not available for printing.

6 From the Vi̲ew menu, choose Sw̲itch Hidden Records.

Choosing this command makes the hidden records the only records that are available for printing. Your screen should look like the following illustration.

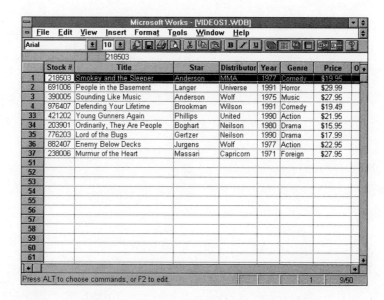

Note There are other ways to select records for printing. In Lesson 11, you'll learn how to use the Find command and queries to select records that match certain conditions.

Preview records before printing

Print Preview

1 Click the Print Preview button on the toolbar.

The selected records appear in the Print Preview window.

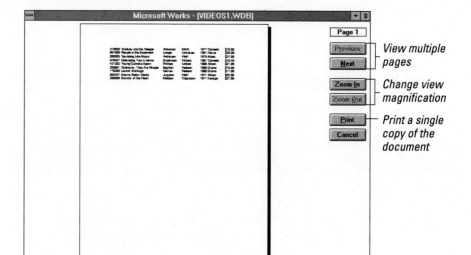

Your data might look better turned horizontally on the page, and the list will be more informative if it includes field names above each column, a descriptive title, and the current date. You can use page setup options to add field names and change the page orientation, and you can use a header and a footer to add a report title and the current date.

2 Click the Cancel button to close the Print Preview window.

Change the page setup

1 From the File menu, choose Page Setup.

The Page Setup dialog box appears showing margin options.

2 Click the Source, Size And Orientation tab.

The current page orientation is portrait (vertical).

3 Under Orientation, select Landscape.

The orientation is now landscape (horizontal). The Sample section illustrates the new orientation.

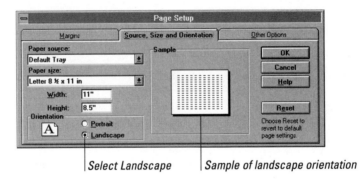

Select Landscape   Sample of landscape orientation

4 Click the Other Options tab.

5 Turn on the Print Record And Field Labels check box.

This specifies that the record and field labels will print. The Other Options tab of the Page Setup dialog box should now match the following illustration.

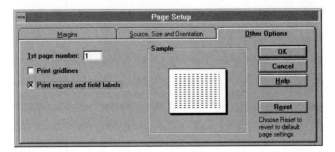

6 Click the OK button.

Print Preview

7 Click the Print Preview button on the toolbar to view the new page setup options. Your screen should now match the following illustration.

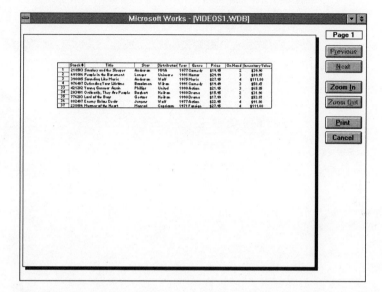

Some of the field names look misproportioned because the letters are so small in Print Preview. Click the field names a couple of times to magnify the view, and you'll see that they look fine.

8 Click the Cancel button to close the Print Preview window.

Add a header and a footer

1 From the View menu, choose Headers And Footers.

The Headers And Footers dialog box appears.

For a complete list of special codes you can use in headers and footers, see the Microsoft Works for Windows User's Guide, Chapter 6, "Creating a header or footer and numbering pages."

2 In the Header text box, type **&cBest Selling Videos**

This header will print the text "Best Selling Videos," centered at the top of the page.

3 Press TAB to move to the Footer text box and then type **&r&d**

This footer will print the current date, right-aligned, at the bottom of the page. The Headers And Footers dialog box should now look like the following.

4 Press ENTER.

Print Preview

5 Click the Print Preview button on the toolbar to view the header and the footer. Your screen should look like the following illustration.

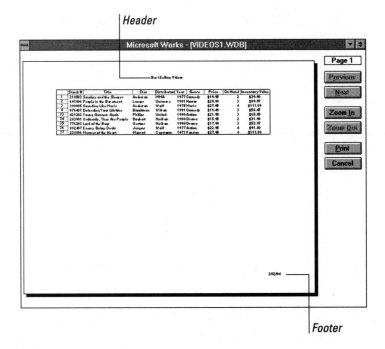

Header

Footer

6 Click the Print button in the Print Preview window to print the list.

Tip If you want to print multiple copies of the report, choose Print from the File menu and specify the number of copies.

Show all records

After you print your report, you need to redisplay all of the database records so they are available for other operations.

Save

1 From the View menu, choose Show All Records.

2 Click the Save button to save your work.

One Step Further

When there are several items to add to your database, you can prepare the information for data entry by writing it on blank database forms. You generate the forms by printing blank records in form view.

Print a blank form

1 Switch to form view.

2 From the File menu, choose Page Setup.

3 Click the Source, Size And Orientation tab.

4 Under Orientation, select Portrait, and then click the OK button.

Portrait orientation is often more appropriate for printing in form view.

5 From the View menu, choose Headers And Footers.

The Headers And Footers dialog box appears. You don't need the header and footer for data entry purposes.

6 Press DELETE, press TAB, press DELETE, and then press ENTER to delete the header and footer text and close the dialog box.

Last Record

7 In the bottom left corner of the database window, click the Last Record button to display a blank record.

8 From the File menu, choose Print.

The Print dialog box appears.

9 Under Print Which Records, select Current Record Only.

The Print dialog box should match the following illustration.

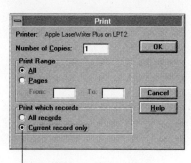

Select Current Record Only

10 Click the OK button to print the blank form.

11 Click the Save button on the toolbar to save your work.

Save

If You Want to Continue to the Next Lesson

▶ Double-click the Document Control-menu box in the menu bar to close VIDEOS1.WDB.

Document Control-menu box

If You Want to Quit Works for Now

▶ Double-click the Application Control-menu box in the title bar.

Application Control-menu box

Lesson Summary

To	Do this	Button
Open an existing database	Click the Open An Existing Document button in the Startup dialog box. In the File Name list box, double-click the name of the database you want to open.	
Insert a field	Position the insertion point, type a field name followed by a colon (:), press ENTER, set the field width and height, and then press ENTER.	
Add a label	Position the insertion point, type the label text, and then press ENTER.	
Move a label or field	Highlight the label or field and then drag it to a new position.	
Save a database	Click the Save button on the toolbar.	
Enter a record	Display a blank record, highlight the first field, and then type each field entry, pressing TAB to move between entries. In list view, press ENTER to move between entries.	
Replace a field entry	Highlight the field containing the entry, type a new entry, and then press ENTER.	
Edit a field entry	Highlight the field containing the entry, click the formula bar, change the entry in the formula bar, and then press ENTER.	
Delete a record	Highlight the record in list view and then choose Delete Record from the Insert menu.	
Undo a change	From the Edit menu, choose Undo.	
Change the size of a field	In form view, highlight the field, choose Field Size from the Format menu, type a new field width, and then press ENTER. In list view, move the highlight to the field you want to change, choose Field Width from the Format menu, type a new field width, and then press ENTER.	

To	Do this	Button
Change a number format	Highlight the fields you want to change, choose Number from the Format menu, select a format, type the number of decimal places, and then press ENTER.	
Change the alignment of field entries	Highlight the fields you want to change, choose Alignment from the Format menu, select an Alignment option, and then click the OK button.	
Change the font of text	Highlight the labels and fields you want to change, click the arrow to the right of the Font Name list box on the toolbar, and then select a font.	`Times New Roman`
Change the font size of text	Highlight the labels and fields you want to change, click the arrow to the right of the Font Size list box on the toolbar, and then select a font size.	`12`
Change the font style of text	Highlight the labels and fields you want to change, and then click the Bold, Italic, or Underline button on the toolbar.	**B** *I* U
Add a border	Highlight the field or label to which you want to add a border, choose Border from the Format menu, select a line style, and then click the OK button.	
Add shading	Highlight the field or label to which you want to add shading, choose Patterns from the Format menu, select a shading pattern from the Pattern list box, and then click the OK button.	
Hide records	Highlight the records in list view and then choose Hide Record from the View menu.	
Switch between hidden and displayed records	From the View menu, choose Switch Hidden Records.	
Show all records	From the View menu, choose Show All Records.	
Preview records	Click the Print Preview button on the toolbar.	

To	Do this	Button
Change the page orientation	From the File menu, choose Page Setup, click the Source, Size And Orientation tab, select an Orientation option, and then click the OK button.	
Print with record and field labels	From the File menu, choose Page Setup, click the Other Options tab, turn on the Print Record And Field Labels check box, and then click the OK button.	
Add a header and a footer	From the View menu, choose Headers And Footers, type the header and footer text and codes, and then press ENTER.	
Print records	Click the Print button on the toolbar.	
Print a blank form	Display a blank record in form view, choose Print from the File menu, select Current Record Only, and then click the OK button.	

For more information on	See in the *Microsoft Works User's Guide*
Creating a database	Chapter 6, "Beginning a database" Chapter 6, "Creating a database form" Chapter 6, "Adding a field" Chapter 6, "Entering labels or descriptive text in a form" Chapter 6, "Positioning and moving fields"
Entering database information	Chapter 6, "Entering information" Chapter 6, "Adding and deleting records in a database" Chapter 6, "Using mathematical formulas and functions to create calculating fields"
Editing database information	Chapter 6, "Making changes to a field entry"
Formatting a database	Chapter 6, "Changing the size of a field or record" Chapter 6, "Changing number formats" Chapter 6, "Changing alignment in a field" Chapter 6, "Changing fonts, font sizes, font styles, and colors" Chapter 6, "Adding a rectangle, borders, colors, and shading to a form"
Printing database records	Chapter 6, "Changing page and margin settings" Chapter 6, "Creating a header or footer and numbering pages" Chapter 11, "Printing with Works"

For online information about	From the Help menu, choose Contents and then
Creating a database	Choose "Database," choose "Database basics," and select the topic "Creating a database in form view."
Entering database information	Choose "Database," choose "Database basics," and select the topic "Adding and deleting records."
Editing database information	Choose "Database," choose "Changing database information," and select the topic "Changing field entries."
Formatting a database	Choose "Database," choose "Changing the appearance of your database," and select a topic.
Printing a database	Choose "Database," choose "Printing a database," and select a topic.

Preview of the Next Lesson

In this lesson, you opened your video inventory database, entered two new records, edited some field entries, formatted the database form, and produced a list of your best selling videos. In the next lesson, you'll learn how to manipulate the information in your database. You'll use the find and replace features to change field entries and you will sort the database records in alphabetical and numerical order. You'll also use queries to select records that match certain conditions.

Manipulating Database Information

You store information in a database so you can view and use the information in different ways. For example, you can use the information in your video inventory database to search for a video title and look up its selling price, arrange and view your list of videos in alphabetical order by title, or produce a report of videos in your inventory grouped by distributor. In fact, there is practically no limit to the ways you can access and use the information stored in a database. In this lesson, you'll learn different ways to access, manipulate, and view the information in your database.

If your screen does not match the illustrations in this lesson, see the Appendix, "Matching the Exercises."

You will learn how to:

- Find and replace database information.
- Sort database records.
- Create and apply queries.

Estimated lesson time: 25 minutes

Start the lesson

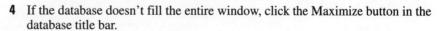

1 In the Startup dialog box, click the Open An Existing Document button.

2 Make sure C:\MSWORKS\WORKSSBS is the current directory.

3 In the File Name list box, double-click 2VIDEOS.WDB.

2VIDEOS.WDB matches the database you worked with at the end of Lesson 9.

4 If the database doesn't fill the entire window, click the Maximize button in the database title bar.

Maximize

5 Save the file as VIDEOS2.WDB.

Finding and Replacing Database Information

You use the find feature to search for database records that have a specific field entry. In form view, you might search for a specific video title and display that record for editing. In list view, you might search for all videos with the same distributor and use the resulting list to produce a simple report.

The replace feature, a companion to the find feature, lets you make global editing changes to your database. For example, you can reduce the price of all $21.95 videos to $19.95 or change the name of the distributor for a group of videos by using a single command.

In the next exercises, you'll use the find and replace features.

Find a record in form view

You want to find the record for the video "Somewhere Out of Time" so you can look up the selling price. Since you are looking for only one record, form view is appropriate.

1 From the Edit menu, choose Find.

The Find dialog box appears.

2 In the Find What text box, type **somewhere out**

These characters are *search characters*, which specify the entry to search for.

The Find dialog box should look like the following.

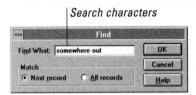

The Next Record option specifies that only the next sequential record containing the search characters will be displayed; the All Records option specifies that all records containing the search characters will be displayed.

Note   The find feature is not case-sensitive, so you don't need to match the capitalization of the text you're searching for. When you type "somewhere out," Works will be able to find "somewhere out," "Somewhere Out," and "SOMEWHERE OUT."

---

3 Press ENTER.

Works finds and displays the next record that contains the search characters.

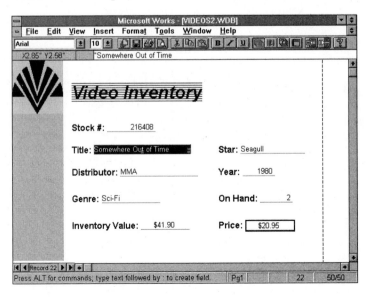

Find records in list view

You know how to find a single record in form view. Now your supervisor has asked you to create a list of all the science fiction videos in your inventory. Since you will need to see a list of records, list view is appropriate for this task.

List View

1   Click the List View button on the toolbar to switch to list view.

2   Click the Genre field name to highlight that field for every record.

When you highlight a field before beginning a search, Works searches only that field, rather than the entire database. If the search characters appear in fields other than the one you highlight, the corresponding record will not be in the list.

3   From the Edit menu, choose Find.

4   Type **sci-fi** in the Find What text box.

5   Under Match, select All Records, and then click the OK button.

Works finds and displays only the records with "Sci-Fi" in the Genre field.

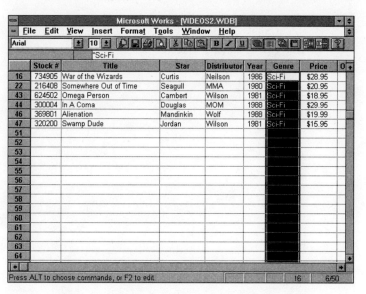

6   Click the Print button on the toolbar to print your list.

Display all the records after a search

Before you conduct another search, you should display all of the database records.

▶   From the View menu, choose Show All Records.

Print

Use a wildcard in a search

Searches don't have to be limited to records containing identical field entries. Your supervisor has requested another list, this time of all the videos in your inventory produced in the 1970s. Since you are looking for years that are similar but not identical, you must use a *wildcard character* when you type your search characters. A wildcard is a single character that takes the place of another character or group of characters.

1   Highlight the Year field for all of the records.

2   From the Edit menu, choose Find.

3   Type **197?** in the Find What text box.

The ? wildcard takes the place of a single character, and specifies that records containing four characters in the Year field, with 197 as the first three characters, will appear in the list.

Note   You can substitute the * wildcard for a group of characters.

---

4   Under Match, select All Records, and then click the OK button.

Works finds and displays the records for the videos produced in the 1970s.

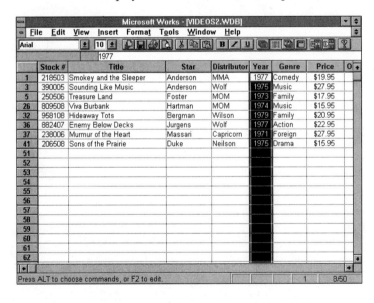

Print

5   Click the Print button on the toolbar to print the list.

Replace information in list view

Two distributors you deal with, Universe and MOM, have merged. As a result, you'll need to replace all occurrences of "MOM" with "Universe" in the Distributor field of your database.

1   From the View menu, choose Show All Records.

2 Highlight the Distributor field for all records.

3 From the Edit menu, choose Replace.

The Replace dialog box appears.

4 Type **mom** in the Find What text box, press TAB to move to the Replace With text box, and then type **Universe**

The Replace dialog box should now appear as shown in the following illustration.

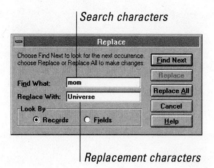

Search characters

Replacement characters

Important   Although the find feature is not case-sensitive, the replacement text you type must exactly match the way you want the text to appear. Works will insert the replacement text exactly as it appears in the Replace With text box.

---

5 Click the Replace All button.

Works replaces all occurrences of "MOM" with "Universe" in the Distributor field.

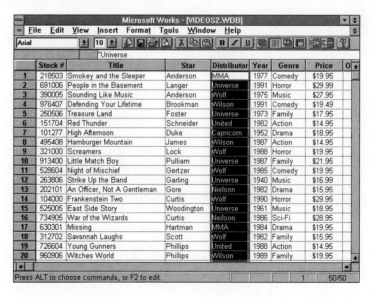

Save

6 Click the Save button on the toolbar to save your work.

Sorting a Database

You can enter information into a database in any order you choose and then arrange, or *sort*, the information in a different order later on. Sorting does not change the contents of your database, but it lets you look at the information in a different way.

When you sort a database, Works changes the order of the records based on the entries in one or more fields. For example, you might sort your video inventory by distributor and video title, specifying the distributor as the first *sort field* and the video title as the second sort field. As a result, the records that include the same distributor will be grouped together and the records will be listed in alphabetical order by video title within each group.

You can sort database records in form view or in list view, although list view is usually more appropriate for viewing records after they are sorted. In the next exercise, you'll sort your video inventory database in list view by distributor and then by video title.

Sort database records

1 From the Tools menu, choose Sort Records.

The Sort Records dialog box appears. In this dialog box, you specify the fields by which the information will be sorted and the order in which the fields will be used.

2 Under 1st Field, click the arrow to the right of the list box, and then select Distributor.

Note   You can sort records in ascending or descending order within each field. Ascending order is A through Z or 0 through 9; descending order is Z through A or 9 through 0.

---

3 Under 2nd Field, click the arrow to the right of the list box, and then select Title.

The Sort Records dialog box should now look like the following illustration.

4 Click the OK button.

The records are now sorted alphabetically by distributor and then by title, as shown in the next illustration.

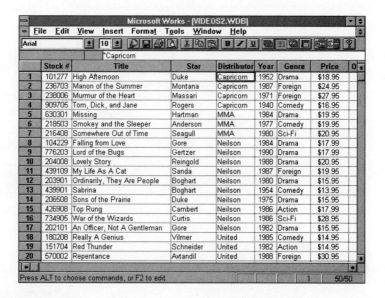

Querying a Database

A *query* is a question you ask about the information stored in a database. You can ask simple questions, such as "Which videos cost $19.95," or more complex ones, such as "Which videos are foreign films produced before 1985 with a selling price between $20.00 and $30.00?" When you query a database, Works searches all the records, selects and displays the ones that match the conditions, and hides the records that do not match.

Using queries, you will be able to help your customers select titles that match their criteria. For example, if a customer wants a list of available horror movies that cost less than $30.00, you can use a query to quickly produce the list.

In the next exercises, you'll use several queries to display information that is often requested by customers or used for generating reports.

Select records that match exactly

The simplest type of query is one that selects records with matching values in a specified field; for example, a list of records with "Duke" in the Star field.

1   From the Tools menu, choose Create New Query.

The New Query dialog box appears.

2   Under Choose A Field To Compare, click the arrow to the right of the A. list box, and then select Star.

Queries are not
case sensitive

3   Under Value To Compare The Field To, click in the E. text box, and then type **duke**

The New Query dialog box should now match the following illustration.

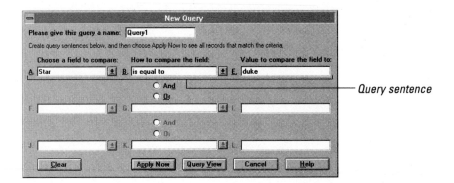

Query sentence

The criteria you have specified comprise a *query sentence*. Works responds to a query sentence by showing all records that match the criteria.

4   Click the Apply Now button.

Works selects and displays only the records with "Duke" in the Star field.

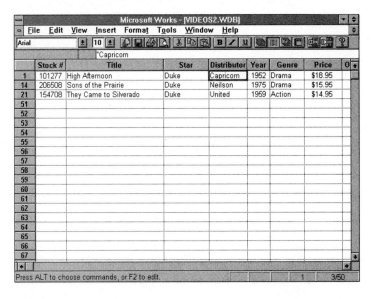

Select records that match in more than one field

Customers often ask you for certain types of videos starring their favorite actors and actresses. Next, you'll list records for all horror videos in which the star is "Curtis."

1   From the Tools menu, choose Create New Query.

2   Click the arrow to the right of the A. list box and then select Star.

3   Click in the E. text box and then type **curtis**

Since this query will find records with matching entries in two fields, you'll need to create a second query sentence.

4 Below the first query sentence, select An**d**.

Selecting this option specifies that the selected records must match the criteria in both query sentences.

5 Click the arrow to the right of the F. list box, scroll down, and then select Genre.

6 Click the arrow to the right of the G. list box and then select Is Equal To.

7 Click in the I. text box and then type **horror**

The New Query dialog box should now match the following illustration.

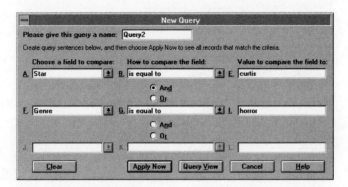

8 Click the Apply Now button.

Works displays the records with "Curtis" in the Star field and "Horror" in the Genre field, as shown in the following illustration.

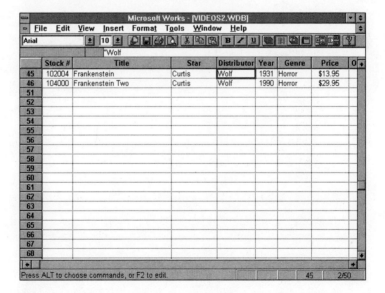

Select records that are above a specified value

When comparing your company's prices to competitors' prices, your supervisor often asks for a list of all videos that sell above a specific price. Next, you'll list records for videos with a selling price of $21.95 or more.

1 From the Tools menu, choose Create New Query.

2 In the A. list box, select Price.

3 In the B. list box, select Is Greater Than Or Equal To.

4 In the E. text box, type **21.95**

The New Query dialog box should look like the following.

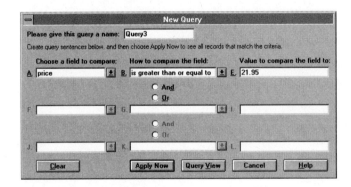

5 Click the Apply Now button.

Works displays the records for videos that sell for $21.95 or more.

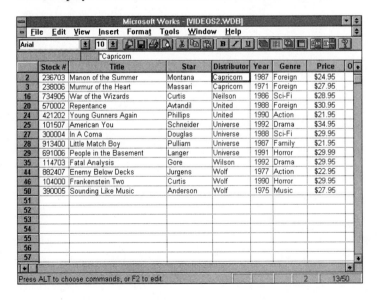

Print

6 Click the Print button on the toolbar to print the results of the query.

Select records that are below a specified value

You can also specify criteria that are less than a specified value. Next, you'll list records for videos with titles that start with the letters "A" through "F."

1 From the Tools menu, choose Create New Query.

2 In the A. list box, select Title.

3 In the B. list box, select Is Less Than.

4 In the E. text box, type **g**

The New Query dialog box should match the next illustration.

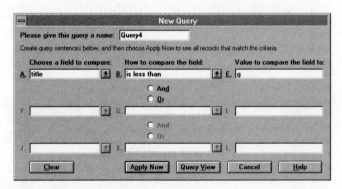

5 Click the Apply Now button.

Works displays the records for videos with titles that start with a letter that precedes the letter "G."

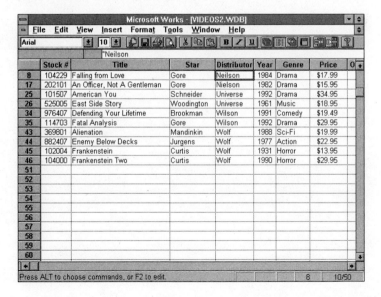

Select records that fall within a range

Customers often want to find videos that sell within a specified price range. Next, you'll list records for videos that are priced from $20.00 through $30.00.

1 From the Tools menu, choose Create New Query.

2 In the A. list box, select Price.

3 In the B. list box, select Is Greater Than Or Equal To.

4 In the E. text box, type **20**

5 Below the first query sentence, select And.

6 In the F. list box, select Price.

7 In the G. list box, select Is Less Than Or Equal To.

8 In the I. text box, type **30**

The New Query dialog box should now look like the following.

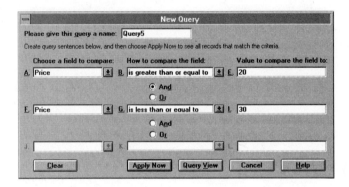

9 Click the Apply Now button.

Works displays the records for videos priced from $20.00 through $30.00, as shown in the following illustration.

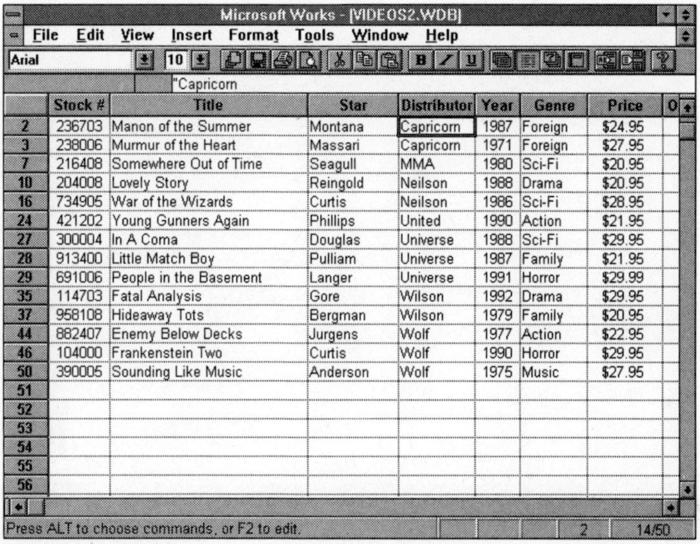
Microsoft Works - [VIDEOS2.WDB]
File Edit View Insert Format Tools Window Help
Arial 10
"Capricorn
Press ALT to choose commands, or F2 to edit.
2 14/50

	Stock #	Title	Star	Distributor	Year	Genre	Price
2	236703	Manon of the Summer	Montana	Capricorn	1987	Foreign	$24.95
3	238006	Murmur of the Heart	Massari	Capricorn	1971	Foreign	$27.95
7	216408	Somewhere Out of Time	Seagull	MMA	1980	Sci-Fi	$20.95
10	204008	Lovely Story	Reingold	Neilson	1988	Drama	$20.95
16	734905	War of the Wizards	Curtis	Neilson	1986	Sci-Fi	$28.95
24	421202	Young Gunners Again	Phillips	United	1990	Action	$21.95
27	300004	In A Coma	Douglas	Universe	1988	Sci-Fi	$29.95
28	913400	Little Match Boy	Pulliam	Universe	1987	Family	$21.95
29	691006	People in the Basement	Langer	Universe	1991	Horror	$29.99
35	114703	Fatal Analysis	Gore	Wilson	1992	Drama	$29.95
37	958108	Hideaway Tots	Bergman	Wilson	1979	Family	$20.95
44	882407	Enemy Below Decks	Jurgens	Wolf	1977	Action	$22.95
46	104000	Frankenstein Two	Curtis	Wolf	1990	Horror	$29.95
50	390005	Sounding Like Music	Anderson	Wolf	1975	Music	$27.95
51							
52							
53							
54							
55							
56							

Print

10 Click the Print button on the toolbar to print the results of the query.

Select records that match any of several conditions

So far, you've used queries to select records that match a single condition or multiple conditions. However, you don't have to limit a query to finding records that match all the conditions specified. You can select records that match any of two or more conditions. For instance, you can list records with either "Curtis" or "Duke" in the Star field.

1 From the Tools menu, choose Create New Query.

2 In the A. list box, select Star.

3 In the E. text box, type **curtis**

4 Below the first query sentence, select Or.

This option specifies that records don't have to match all the conditions to be displayed in the list.

5 In the F. list box, select Star.

6 In the G. list box, select Is Equal To.

7 In the I. text box, type **duke**

The New Query dialog box should now look like the following illustration.

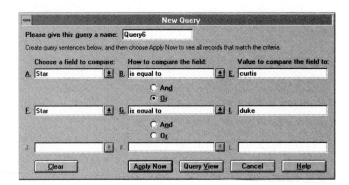

8   Click the Apply Now button.

Works displays the records with either "Curtis" or "Duke" in the Star field.

	Stock #	Title	Star	Distributor	Year	Genre	Price	O
1	101277	High Afternoon	Duke	Capricorn	1952	Drama	$18.95	
14	206508	Sons of the Prairie	Duke	Neilson	1975	Drama	$15.95	
16	734905	War of the Wizards	Curtis	Neilson	1986	Sci-Fi	$28.95	
21	154708	They Came to Silverado	Duke	United	1959	Action	$14.95	
45	102004	Frankenstein	Curtis	Wolf	1931	Horror	$13.95	
46	104000	Frankenstein Two	Curtis	Wolf	1990	Horror	$29.95	
51								
52								
53								
54								
55								
56								
57								
58								
59								
60								
61								
62								
63								
64								

Print

9   Click the Print button on the toolbar to print the results of the query.

Select records using wildcards

For your next query, you'll list records for videos that contain the word "love" in the title. You will need to use the * wildcard character.

1   From the Tools menu, choose Create New Query.

2   In the A. list box, select Title.

3   In the E. text box, type ***love***

The * wildcard character is used in place of a group of characters. By typing "*love*" you specify that any group of characters can appear before or after the word "love."

The New Query dialog box should now appear as follows.

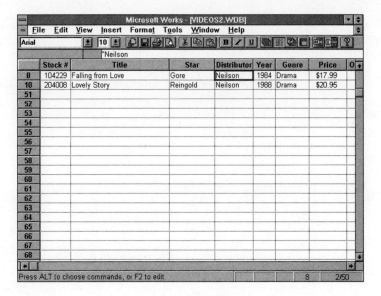

4 Click the Apply Now button.

Works displays the records for videos that contain "love" anywhere in the title.

One Step Further

You can specify as many as three conditions in the New Query dialog box. If you need to create a query that contains more than three conditions or that uses a formula, you will need to create your query in *query view*. Query view allows you to use formulas and functions that you cannot enter in the New Query dialog box. For example, there is no place to enter a function in the New Query dialog box, but in query view you can use a function as part of a query. In the next exercise, you'll use a function to list records for videos with a price of approximately $19. You'll also name queries and apply a previously created query.

Select records using a formula

Query View

1   Click the Query View button on the toolbar.

Works switches to query view, as shown in the next illustration.

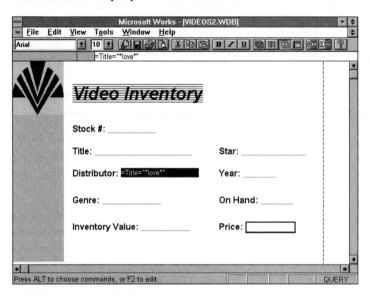

See Appendix A, "Spreadsheet and Database functions," in the Microsoft Works for Windows User's Guide for a description and example of each Works function.

A record viewed in query view looks like a blank record in form view. In query view, you specify conditions by entering values, formulas, or functions in the fields on the form.

2   Press DELETE to clear the entry in the Distributor field.

3   Click the Price field to highlight it.

4   Type **=round(price,0)=19**

This function will round off entries in the Price field with no decimals. Any price between $18.50 and $19.49 will be included in the query result. Works will round values between $18.50 and $18.99 up to $19.00 and will round values between $19.01 and $19.49 down to $19.00.

5   Press ENTER to apply the function.

List View

6   Click the List View button on the toolbar to view the results of the query.

Works applies the query and displays the records for which the Price field entry is approximately $19. Your screen should look like the following illustration.

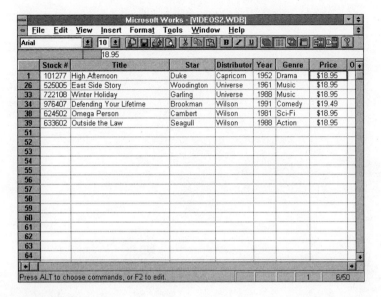

Name queries

If you want to use the same query again in the future, for example as the basis for a custom report, you should give the query a descriptive name. A query name can contain as many as 15 characters.

1   From the Tools menu, choose Name Query.

The Name Query dialog box appears, listing the seven unnamed queries you've created so far. Query7 is highlighted. This is the last query you created, which lists videos that cost approximately $19.00.

2   Click in the Name text box and then type **$19 videos**

The Name Query dialog box should now appear as shown in the next illustration.

3   Click the Rename button to rename "Query7" as "$19 videos."

Note   You can name a query in list view or in query view.

---

4   In the Queries list box, select Query5.

This is the query that lists videos that cost from $20.00 through $30.00.

5   In the Name text box, click to the right of "videos."

6   Press BACKSPACE nine times to delete everything but the leading dollar sign.

7   Type **20-$30 videos**

8   Click the Rename button.

The Name Query dialog box should look like the following illustration.

9   Click the OK button to close the Name Query dialog box.

Save

10 Click the Save button on the toolbar to save your work.

Apply a previously created query

After you name a query, you can apply it at any time rather than recreating the query every time you want to use it.

1   From the View menu, choose Query.

The Queries dialog box appears with a list of available queries.

2   In the Query list box, double-click "$20-$30 videos."

The query view for the $20-$30 videos query appears.

List View

3   Click the List View button on the toolbar to view the results of the query.

Works displays the records for videos priced between $20 and $30.

4   Save your work.

If You Want to Continue to the Next Lesson

Document
Control-menu box

▶ Double-click the Document Control-menu box in the menu bar to close VIDEOS2.WDB.

*Application
Control-menu box*

If You Want to Quit Works for Now

▶ Double-click the Application Control-menu box in the title bar.

Lesson Summary

To	Do this	Button
Find a record	From the Edit menu, choose Find, type the characters you want to find, and then press ENTER.	
Display all records after a search	From the View menu, choose Show All Records.	
Replace information	From the Edit menu, choose Replace, type the characters you want to find, press TAB, type the replacement characters, and then click the Replace All button.	
Sort database records	From the Tools menu, choose Sort Records, select the fields by which you want to sort, select Ascend or Descend for each field, and then click the OK button.	
Create and apply a query with as many as three conditions	From the Tools menu, choose Create New Query, specify as many as three query sentences, and then click the Apply Now button.	
Create and apply a query with more than three conditions or with formulas and functions	Click the Query View button on the toolbar, enter conditions, formulas, or functions in the fields on the form, and then click the List View button on the toolbar.	
Name a query	From the Tools menu, choose Name Query, select a name in the Queries list box, type a new name in the Name text box, click the Rename button, and then click the OK button.	
Apply a previously created query	From the View menu, choose Query, double-click the name of the query you want to apply, and then click the List View button on the toolbar.	

For more information on	See in the *Microsoft Works User's Guide*
Finding and replacing database information	Chapter 6, "Finding and replacing specific text and values"
Sorting database records	Chapter 6, "Organizing your records in alphabetical or numerical order"
Querying a database	Chapter 6, "What is querying?" Chapter 6, "Querying based on up to three criteria" Chapter 6, "Querying based on more than three criteria"

For online information about	From the Help menu, choose Contents and then
Finding and replacing database information	Choose "Database," choose "Database basics," and select the topic "Replacing specific information in the Database."
Sorting database records	Choose "Database," choose "Changing the appearance of your database," and select the topic "Sorting a database."
Querying a database	Choose "Database," choose "Database basics," and select the topic "Selecting which records to view or print."

Preview of the Next Lesson

In the next lesson, you'll learn how to use the Database Reporting feature to create a customized database report. You'll create a standard report, modify text and report instructions to create a customized report, and format and print the report.

Getting Started with Database Reporting

In Lesson 10, you learned how to create lists of specified database records. If you want to create reports with design and content flexibility, you can use the Database Reporting feature. With Database Reporting, you can specify which fields you want to include in a report; add titles, subtitles, and explanatory notes; sort and group information; and show statistical information such as subtotals and totals.

In response to a request from your supervisor, you need to produce a customized report from your video inventory database. The report will need to include only the title, star, price, and on hand quantity of each video, grouped by genre and sorted by title within each group. You will also show a total of the on hand quantity for the videos in each genre group. The following illustration shows what your finished report will look like.

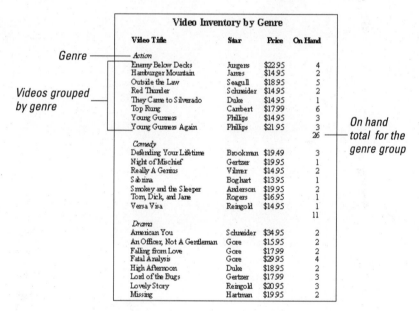

In this lesson, you'll use the Database Reporting feature to create the report.

If your screen does not match the illustrations in this lesson, see the Appendix, "Matching the Exercises."

You will learn how to:

- Create a standard database report.
- Modify a standard report.
- Format a database report.
- Print a database report.

Estimated lesson time: 20 minutes

Start the lesson

1 In the Startup dialog box, click the Open An Existing Document button.

2 Make sure C:\MSWORKS\WORKSSBS is the current directory.

3 In the File Name list box, double-click 3VIDEOS.WDB.

3VIDEOS.WDB matches the database you worked with at the end of Lesson 10.

Maximize

4 If the database doesn't fill the entire window, click the Maximize button in the database title bar.

5 Save the file as VIDEOS3.WDB.

Beginning a Database Report

You begin a database report by creating a *standard report*. A standard report contains a report title, the fields you want to include in the report, and report statistics. When you create a standard report, Works steps you through the process of specifying the report title, fields, and statistics. In the next exercise, you'll create a standard report.

Create a standard report

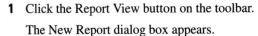

Report View

1 Click the Report View button on the toolbar.

The New Report dialog box appears.

2 In the Report Title text box, type **Video Inventory by Genre**

This title will appear at the top of your report.

3 In the Field list box, select Title, and then click the Add >> button.

The Title field name is added to the Fields In Report list box, which indicates the fields that will be included in the report.

Tip   You can click the Add All >> button to include all of the fields in a report.

---

4 Click the Add >> button to include the Star field in the report.

5 In the Field list box, select Price, and then click the Add >> button.

6 Click the Add >> button to include the On Hand field in the report.

The New Report dialog box should now match the following illustration.

Available fields

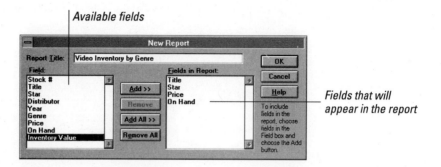

Fields that will
appear in the report

Note   If you make a mistake or change your mind, you can highlight a field in the Fields In Report list box and click the Remove button to remove it. You can click the Remove All button to remove all of the fields and start over.

7   Click the OK button.

The Report Statistics dialog box appears, as shown in the next illustration.

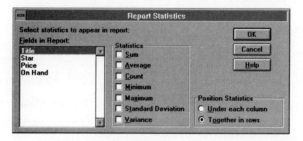

In the Report Statistics dialog box, you can specify functions you want to apply to certain fields. Since your report will show a total of the on hand quantity for each genre group, you will specify the SUM function for the On Hand field.

8   In the Fields In Report list box, select On Hand.

9   Under Statistics, turn on the Sum check box.

This specifies that Works should total the values in the On Hand field.

10   Under Position Statistics, select Under Each Column.

The total will appear under the On Hand column in the report. When you group the videos by genre (as you will do in the next exercise), each group will show an on hand total.

Note   If you select Together In Rows, the statistics will be grouped in a small table at the end of the report, and will not appear within each group.

The Report Statistics dialog box should match the following illustration.

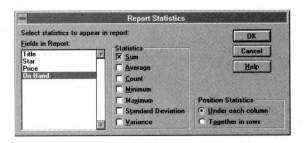

11 Click the OK button.

A message box appears indicating that the report definition has been created.

12 Click the OK button to view the report definition.

The report definition appears in *report view*, as shown in the next illustration.

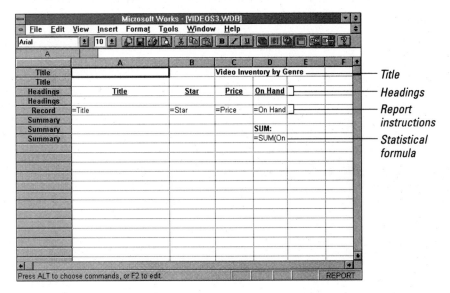

In report view, you see titles, headings, report instructions, and statistical formulas. The report instructions (=Title, =Star, =Price, and =On Hand) specify that the Title, Star, Price, and On Hand field entries for each record will appear in the report. The statistical formula [=SUM(On Hand)] is the formula that will total the on hand values.

You can use Print Preview to see what the report will look like when you print it.

Print Preview

13   Click the Print Preview button on the toolbar and then click the Zoom In button.

In Print Preview, you still see the title and headings, but the report instructions are replaced by the contents of the specified fields and the formula is replaced by the formula result for each record. Your report in Print Preview should now look like the following illustration.

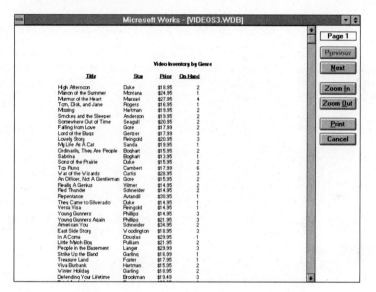

14   Click the Cancel button to close the Print Preview window.

Modifying a Database Report

In many cases, you might find that your standard report is all you need to effectively present your data. However, if the standard report is not exactly what you want, you can modify it in report view.

In the next exercises, you'll sort and group the data in your report and modify some text and report instructions.

Sort and group report information

So far, you have specified the title, fields, and statistical formula you need and have generated a standard report. However, the data in your report still needs to be grouped alphabetically by genre and sorted alphabetically by title within each group, as your supervisor requested. After you sort and group the report data, you can also add some text or instructions to clarify and enhance the data in each group.

1 From the Tools menu, choose Sort Records.

The Sort Records dialog box appears.

2 Under 1st Field, click the arrow to the right of the list box, scroll down, and then select Genre.

This specifies that the data will be sorted by genre.

3 Under 1st Field, turn on the Break G check box.

Turning on this check box specifies that the report information will be grouped by genre type. Works will insert a Summ Genre row in the report definition that will produce a group total at the end of each genre group. Summ Genre stands for Summary of Genre.

Note   The letters that appear next to the option buttons and check boxes in the Sort Records dialog box represent keys that you can press while holding down the ALT key if you want to select the options using the keyboard.

---

4 Under 2nd Field, click the arrow to the right of the list box, and then select Title.

Within each genre group, the report information will be sorted by title. The Sort Records dialog box should now look like the next illustration.

5 Click the OK button.

Works adds a Summ Genre row to the report definition, as shown in the following illustration.

Works inserts a Summ Genre row

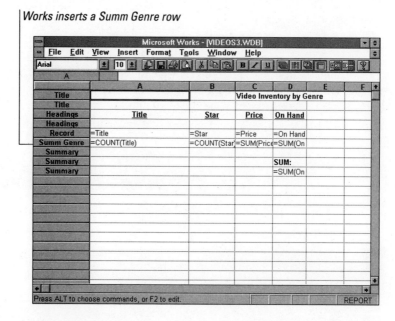

The Summ Genre row groups the report information by each genre type. This row can contain text or formulas for information that you want to show after each group. Initially, the Summ Genre row contains calculation formulas for each column. For fields with text entries, the number of entries will be counted. For fields with numeric values, the total of the values for each column will be summed.

Print Preview

6 Click the Print Preview button on the toolbar and then click the Zoom In button.

The current report definition groups the records as shown in the next illustration.

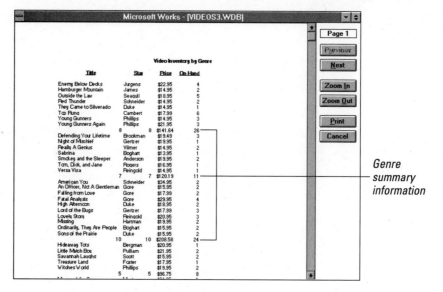

Genre summary information

7 Click the Print button in the Print Preview window to print the report.

Add a group heading

Right now the records in your report are grouped, but there is nothing in the report to indicate that they are grouped by genre. You can clarify this information by showing the genre name at the beginning of each group of records. To do this, you'll need to insert a row and add a report instruction.

1 Click the row label in the first title row to highlight the row.

Click here to highlight the first Title row

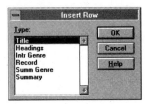

	A	B	C	D	E	F
Title		Video Inventory by Genre				
Title						
Headings	Title	Star	Price	On Hand		
Headings						
Record	=Title	=Star	=Price	=On Hand		
Summ Genre	=COUNT(Title)	=COUNT(Star)	=SUM(Price	=SUM(On		
Summary						
Summary				SUM:		
Summary				=SUM(On		

2 From the Insert menu, choose Row/Column.

The Insert Row dialog box appears so you can select the type of row to insert.

3 In the Type list box, double-click Intr Genre.

Works inserts a blank Intr Genre row in the report definition. Intr Genre stands for Introduction of Genre. The Intr Genre row allows you to insert text, fields, or formulas that will appear at the beginning of each genre group.

4 Type **=Genre** and then press ENTER.

The text "=Genre" instructs Works to show the genre name at the beginning of each group. Your screen should now look like the following illustration.

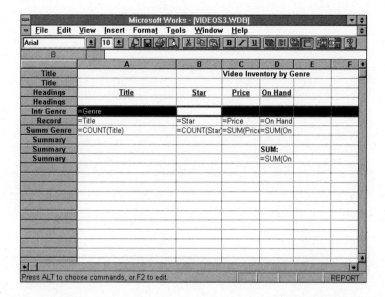

Print Preview

5 Click the Print Preview button on the toolbar and then click the Zoom In button. Now a genre name appears at the beginning of each group.

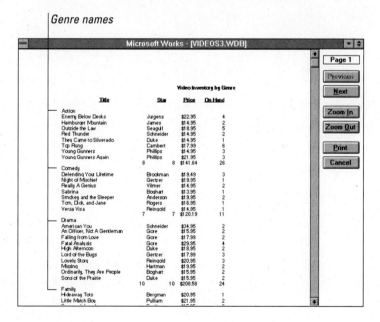

6 Click the Cancel button to close the Print Preview window.

Change a heading

You don't have to use the field names from the database as the column headings for your report. You decide to make the first column heading more descriptive.

1 In the first Headings row, move the highlight to the "Title" heading.

2 Type **Video Title** and then press ENTER.

Your screen should now look like the following illustration.

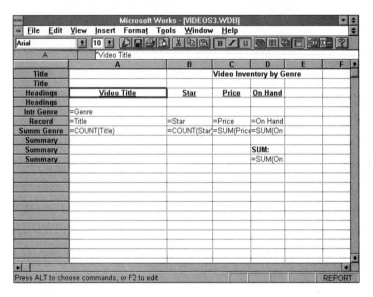

Delete report instructions

Your report currently shows totals for all of the columns. Since your supervisor requested a total only in the On Hand column, you need to delete all of the calculation formulas in the Summ Genre row except the =SUM(On Hand) calculation formula.

1 In the Summ Genre row, highlight the calculation formulas in columns A, B, and C.

2 Press DELETE to delete the formulas.

The report definition should now look like the following illustration.

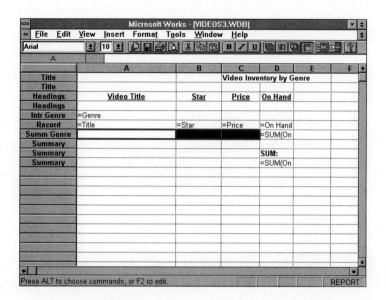

Print Preview

3 Click the Print Preview button on the toolbar and then click the Zoom In button.

The report now shows only an On Hand total for each genre group. Your report should now match the following illustration.

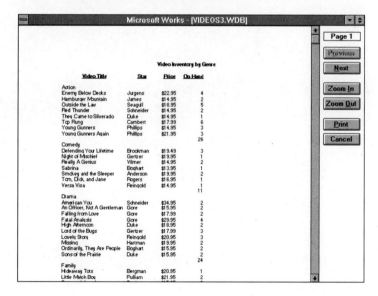

4 Click the Cancel button to close the Print Preview window.

Formatting a Database Report

Now that you've specified all of the information that will appear in your report, you can apply formatting features to make the report more attractive and easier to read. In the next exercises, you'll format your database report.

Change the font, size, and style of text

As with any Works document, you can change the font, size, and style of text in a database report.

1   Click the box to the left of column A and above the first Title row label.

The entire report definition should now be highlighted, as shown in the next illustration.

Click here to highlight the entire report definition

	A	B	C	D	E	F
Title			Video Inventory by Genre			
Title						
Headings	Video Title	Star	Price	On Hand		
Headings						
Intr Genre	=Genre					
Record	=Title	=Star	=Price	=On Hand		
Summ Genre				=SUM(On		
Summary						
Summary				SUM:		
Summary				=SUM(On		

Microsoft Works - [VIDEOS3.WDB]

File   Edit   View   Insert   Format   Tools   Window   Help

Press ALT to choose commands, or F2 to edit.   REPORT

Font Name list box

Font Size list box

2   Click the arrow to the right of the Font Name list box on the toolbar and select Times New Roman.

3   Click the arrow to the right of the Font Size list box on the toolbar and select 12.

All the text in the report definition now appears in the Times New Roman 12-point font.

4   In the first Title row, click in column C.

The title "Video Inventory by Genre" is highlighted.

5   Click the arrow to the right of the Font Size list box on the toolbar and select 16.

6   Click the "=Genre" report instruction in column A to highlight it.

Italic

7   Click the Italic button on the toolbar.

By italicizing the report instruction, you specify that the genre name at the beginning of each group in the database report will be italicized.

Your screen should now look like the following illustration.

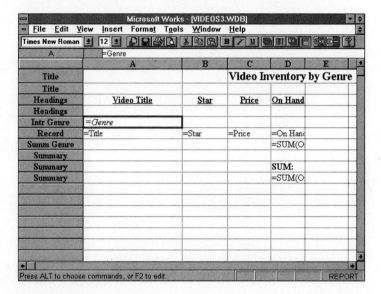

Change column widths

In its current form, your report is difficult to read because the columns of information are very close to each other. You can change column widths to add space between the columns of your report.

1   Be sure the highlight is in column A.

2   From the Format menu, choose Column Width.

The Column Width dialog box appears.

3   Type **30** and then press ENTER.

The column width increases to 30 characters.

4   Drag across column labels C and D to highlight the columns.

5   From the Format menu, choose Column Width.

6   Type **10** if that is not the number that currently appears in the Width text box, and then press ENTER.

Both columns are now 10 characters wide. Your screen should now match the following illustration.

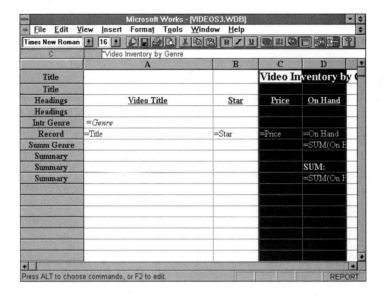

Change the alignment of entries

To further enhance the appearance of your report, you can center the report title over the columns of information and change the alignment of the "Video Title" and "Star" headings.

1 Click the title "Video Inventory by Genre" to highlight it.

Cut

2 Click the Cut button on the toolbar to remove the title and place it in the Clipboard.

3 In the first Title row, move the highlight to column A.

Paste

4 Click the Paste button on the toolbar to paste the title in the new location.

5 In the first Title row, highlight columns A through D.

6 From the Format menu, choose Alignment.

The Alignment dialog box appears.

7 Under Alignment, select Center Across Selection, and then click the OK button.

The title is centered across the highlighted range.

8 In the first Headings row, highlight the headings "Video Title" and "Star."

9 From the Format menu, choose Alignment.

10 Under Alignment, select Left, and then click the OK button.

Your screen should look like the following.

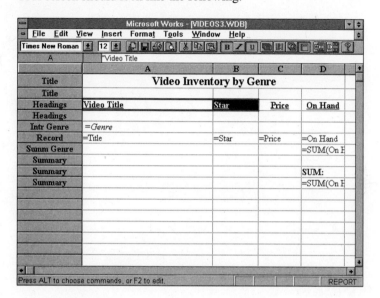

Change margins

You can make your report information look more balanced by changing the margins of the report definition.

1 From the File menu, choose Page Setup.

The Page Setup dialog box appears.

2 Click the Margins tab if it isn't the displayed tab.

3 Double-click in the Left Margin text box and then type **1.5**

4 Press TAB to move to the Right Margin text box, type **1.5**, and then press ENTER.

Print Preview

5 Click the Print Preview button on the toolbar and then click the Zoom In button.

The current report definition generates the report shown in the next illustration.

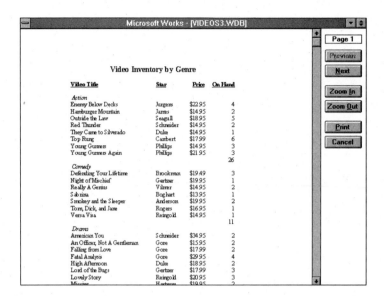

6 Click the Cancel button to close the Print Preview window.

7 Save your work.

Printing a Database Report

Now that your report looks the way you want it and contains all of the information you want to present, you can print it. However, since the report is two pages long, you might want to first add page numbers to the bottom of each page. In the next exercises, you'll add a footer to number the pages and you'll print the report.

Add a footer

1 From the View menu, choose Headers And Footers.

The Headers And Footers dialog box appears.

For a complete list of special codes you can use in headers and footers, see the Microsoft Works for Windows User's Guide, Chapter 6, "Creating a header or footer and numbering pages."

2 Press TAB to move to the Footer text box and then type **&c&p**

This footer will place a centered page number at the bottom of each page. The Headers And Footers dialog box should look like the following.

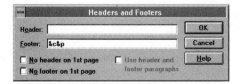

NB footer margin may need to be changed – 1" will m

Print Preview

3 Press ENTER.

4 Click the Print Preview button on the toolbar.

5 Click the Next button to view the second page.

A centered page number appears at the bottom of each page.

6 Click the Cancel button to close the Print Preview window.

Print the report

Print

1 Click the Print button on the toolbar.

Tip If you want to print multiple copies of a report, choose Print from the File menu and specify the number of copies to print.

Save

2 Click the Save button on the toolbar.

The report definition is saved with the database.

One Step Further

When you print a report, you can include all of the database records or you can use a query to select only certain records. Currently, your report includes all of the database records. Your supervisor has now asked you to include only the records for videos produced in 1988 or later. In the next exercise, you'll accomplish this task by creating a query and basing your report on the results of the query. You'll also give your report a descriptive name.

Base a report on the results of a query

1 From the Tools menu, choose Create New Query.

The New Query dialog box appears.

2 Click the arrow to the right of the A. list box and then select Year.

3 Click the arrow to the right of the B. list box and then select Is Greater Than.

4 Click in the E. text box and then type **1987**

5 Click the Apply Now button.

Works applies the query and returns to the report definition.

Print Preview

6 Click the Print Preview button on the toolbar.

The report now includes only the records for videos produced in 1988 or later, as shown in the following illustration.

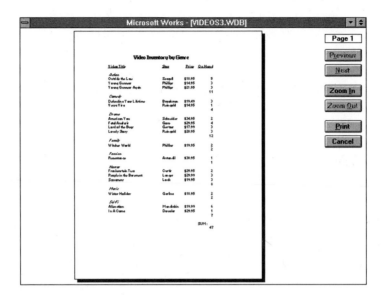

7   Click the Cancel button to close the Print Preview window.

Name the report

1   From the Tools menu, choose Name Report.

The Name Report dialog box appears showing Report1, which is your unnamed report.

2   Click in the Name text box and then type **Videos by Genre**

The Name Report dialog box should now look like the following.

3   Click the Rename button to assign the name to the report.

4   Click the OK button to close the Name Report dialog box.

Tip   To access the report at a later time, choose Report from the View menu and then select the report name.

---

5   Click the Save button on the toolbar to save your work.

Save

Document Control-menu box

Application Control-menu box

If You Want to Continue to the Next Lesson

▶ Double-click the Document Control-menu box in the menu bar.

If You Want to Quit Works for Now

▶ Double-click the Application Control-menu box in the title bar.

Lesson Summary

To	Do this	Button
Create a standard report	From the Tools menu, choose Create New Report, type a report title, select the fields you want to include in the report, and then click the OK button. Specify the statistics you want to include in the report, select the position of the statistics, click the OK button to create the report definition, and then click the OK button to close the message box.	
Sort and group records in a report	From the Tools menu, choose Sort Records, select as many as three fields by which to sort the report, turn on the Break option under the field which you will use to group the records, and then click the OK button.	
Add a group heading	Highlight a row in the report definition, choose Row/Column from the Insert menu, double-click the Intr *fieldname* row type, and then enter the information you want to appear as a group heading in the Intr *fieldname* row.	
Delete a report instruction	Highlight the instruction and then press DELETE.	
Change the font of text	Highlight the entries you want to change, click the arrow to the right of the Font Name list on the toolbar, and then select a new font.	Arial ▼
Change the font size of text	Highlight the entries you want to change, click the arrow to the right of the Font Size list box on the toolbar, and then select a new font size.	10 ▼

To	Do this	Button
Change the font style of text	Highlight the entries you want to change and then click the Bold, Italic, or Underline button on the toolbar.	**B** / **U**
Change a column width	Highlight the column you want to change, choose Column Width from the Format menu, type a new width, and then press ENTER.	
Change the alignment of entries	Highlight the entries you want to change, choose Alignment from the Format menu, select a new alignment, and then click the OK button.	
Change margins	From the File menu, choose Page Setup, click the Margins tab, enter new margin settings, and then press ENTER.	
Add a footer	From the View menu, choose Headers And Footers, type text and codes in the Footer text box, and then press ENTER.	
Preview a report	Click the Print Preview button on the toolbar.	
Print a report	Click the Print button on the toolbar.	

For more information on	See in the *Microsoft Works User's Guide*
Creating a standard report	Chapter 7, "Beginning a Database report" Chapter 7, "Understanding the report definition"
Modifying a database report	Chapter 7, "Sorting and grouping field entries" Chapter 7, "Adding and deleting rows and columns" Chapter 7, "Changing and deleting entries" Chapter 7, "Adding titles, headings, and labels to a report" Chapter 7, "Adding instructions for report contents and calculations"
Formatting a database report	Chapter 7, "Changing column width and row height" Chapter 7, "Changing number formats" Chapter 7, "Changing alignment in a field" Chapter 7, "Changing fonts, font sizes, font styles, and colors" Chapter 7, "Changing page and margin settings"

For more information on	See in the *Microsoft Works User's Guide*
Printing a database report	Chapter 7, "Creating a header or footer and numbering pages"
	Chapter 11, "Printing with Works"

For online information about	From the Help menu, choose Contents and then
Creating a report	Choose "Reporting," choose "Reporting basics," and select the topic "Creating a report."
Modifying a database report	Choose "Reporting," choose "Changing report information," and select a topic.
Formatting a database report	Choose "Reporting," choose "Changing the appearance of your report," and select a topic.
Printing a database report	Choose "Reporting," choose "Printing a report," and select the topic "Printing reports."

Preview of the Next Lessons

In Part 4 of this book, you'll learn how to use the Communications tool. You'll start a Communications session, connect and reconnect to another computer, and quit a Communications session. You'll also transfer files from one computer to another and automate connections between computers.

Review & Practice

In the lessons in Part 3, "Using the Database," you learned how to create, edit, and format database files. You also learned how to find, sort, and query database information and use the Database Reporting feature to create customized reports. If you want to practice these skills and test your understanding before you proceed with the next lesson, you can work through the Review & Practice section following this lesson.

Part 3   Review & Practice

Before you begin learning how to use the Communications tool, practice the skills you learned in Part 3 by working through this Review & Practice section. You'll use the Database tool to modify and format a database. You'll also find and replace field entries, sort records, create queries, create and print a database report, and print database records.

Scenario

In the last few weeks you have impressed upper management with your database abilities. As a result, you've been asked to lend a hand to the new merchandise control manager at West Coast Sales's parent company, which sells a wide range of home and office products. The merchandise control department keeps detailed records of products, cost, price, and on hand quantities in inventory. There is a separate Works database file for each group of products. For example, data for appliances is stored in one file and data for home furnishings is stored in another.

With the new wave of in-home offices, the company has decided to offer a new line of affordable office supplies and products to its customers. The manager of the merchandise control department has set up a database to store the information for this new product group. You've been asked to modify and format the database and set up some initial queries and a database report.

You will review and practice how to:

- Modify a database.
- Format a database.
- Manipulate database information.
- Create a database report.
- Print database information.

Estimated practice time: 30 minutes

Step 1: Modify a Database

In this step, you'll add a field that calculates inventory value, change a field name, and change field sizes.

Add a field

1   Open the 2OFFICE.WDB database from the MSWORKS\WORKSSBS directory.

2 Maximize the database window if it isn't already maximized.

3 Save the database as OFFICE2.WDB.

4 Switch to form view and then add the field shown in the following table.

Position	Field Name	Width	Height
X5.08" Y3.25"	Inventory Value:	14	1

Enter a formula

1 Highlight the Inventory Value field.

2 Enter a formula that multiplies the value in the Price field by the value in the On Hand field.

Change a field name

▶ Highlight the Group: field name and then change the name to "Category:" Be sure to press ENTER or click the Enter box in the formula bar to complete the step.

Your screen should look like the following.

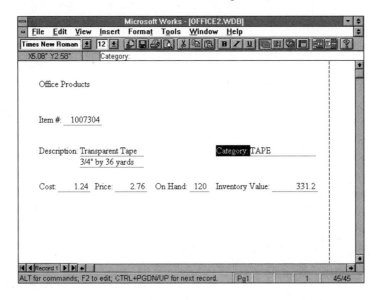

Change field sizes

1 Highlight the Description field.

2 Open the Field Size dialog box and then change the field width to 40 and the field height to 1.

3 Switch to list view, change the width of the Description field to Best Fit, and then change the width of the Category field to 15.

4 Save OFFICE2.WDB.

For more information on	See
Adding fields	Lesson 9
Entering formulas	Lesson 9
Changing field names	Lesson 9
Changing field sizes	Lesson 9

Step 2: Format a Database

In this step, you'll change the font, size, and style of text; change number formats; change the alignment of entries; and add borders.

Change the font, size, and style of text

1 Switch to form view and then highlight all of the field names, fields, and labels on the database form.

2 Change the font to Arial and the font size to 10.

3 Highlight the "Office Products" label.

4 Change the font size to 20 and the font style to Bold.

5 Highlight all of the field names on the database form and then change the font style to Bold.

Change the number format

1 Highlight the Cost, Price, and Inventory Value fields.

2 Open the Number dialog box and then change the format to Currency with two decimals.

Change the alignment of entries

1 Highlight the Item #, Category, and Inventory Value fields.

2 Open the Alignment dialog box and then center the field entries.

Add borders

1 Highlight the Description field.

2 Open the Border dialog box and then add a thin outline border to the field.

3 Click a blank area in the form view window.

4 Save OFFICE2.WDB.

Your database form should now look like the one in the following illustration.

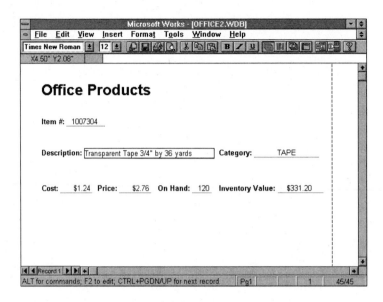

For more information on	See
Changing the font, size, and style of text	Lesson 9
Changing the number format	Lesson 9
Changing the alignment of entries	Lesson 9
Adding borders	Lesson 9

Step 3: Manipulate Database Information

In this step, you'll find and replace field entries, sort records, and query the database.

Find and replace field entries

1 Change to list view.

2 In the Category field, find "PENS/PENCILS" and replace all occurrences with "WRITING TOOLS."

Sort records

1 Open the Sort Records dialog box.

2 Sort the records in ascending order by Category and Description.

Your report definition should match the following illustration.

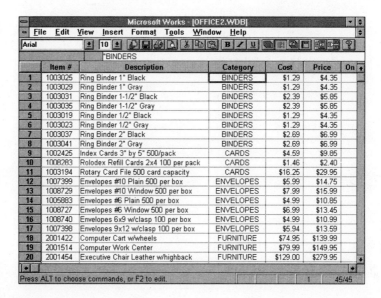

Query a database

1 Create and apply a query to select records with a Price field entry greater than $29.

2 Name the current query "Price over $29."

3 Switch to query view and then enter a formula in the Price field that selects records in which Price minus Cost is less than $2.

4 Switch to list view to see the result of the formula.

Your screen should now look like the following illustration.

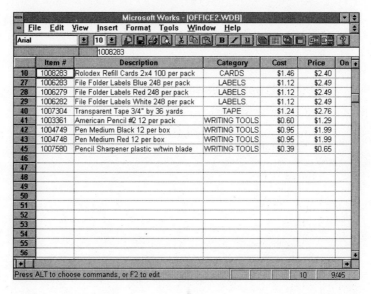

5 Create and apply a query that selects records for which the category is not FURNITURE, BINDERS, or WRITING TOOLS.

6 Name the current query "Paper Products."

7 Show all of the database records.

8 Save OFFICE2.WDB.

For more information on	See
Finding and replacing field entries	Lesson 10
Sorting records	Lesson 10
Querying a database	Lesson 10

Step 4: Create a Database Report

In this step, you'll create a standard report; sort and group field entries; insert rows; modify titles, headings, labels, and report instructions; and format the database report.

Create a standard report

1 Apply the Paper Products query.

2 Open the New Report dialog box and type the report title "Paper Products."

3 Add the Description, Price, On Hand, and Inventory Value fields to the report.

4 Total the Inventory Value field in a row at the end of each category.

5 Display the report definition.

Your report definition should look like the following.

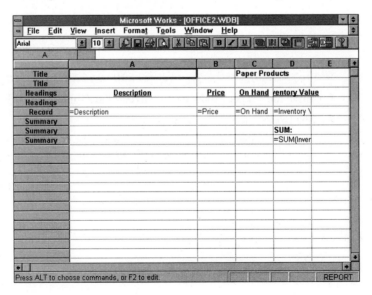

Sort and group field entries

1 Open the Sort Records dialog box.

2 Sort and group the records in ascending order by category and then by description.

3 Preview the report.

Your report should match the following illustration.

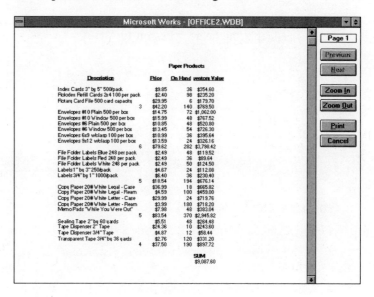

Insert rows

1 Highlight the Summ Category row and then insert another Summ Category row.

2 Insert another Summ Category row above the first Summary row.

3 Insert an Intr Category row.

Modify titles, headings, labels, and report instructions

1 Move the "Paper Products" title to column A in the first Title row.

2 Change the "Inventory Value" heading to "Inv Value."

3 Move to column A in the Intr Category row and then insert a field entry instruction that will show the category name at the beginning of each group.

4 Delete the "=COUNT(Description)", "=SUM(Price)", and "=SUM(On Hand)" calculation formulas in the second Summ Category row.

5 Add the label "Category Total" in column A in the second Summ Category row.

Your report definition should now look like the following illustration.

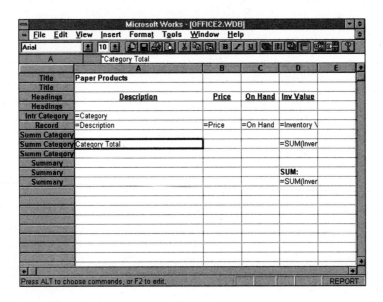

Format a database report

1 Highlight the "Paper Products" title and then change the font size to 16.

2 Highlight the "=Category" field entry instruction and then change the font style to Bold.

3 Center the field entry instruction in the On Hand column.

4 Right-align the field entry instruction and calculation formula in the Inv Value column.

5 Center the "Category Total" label in column A in the second Summ Category row.

Your report definition should now look like the following illustration.

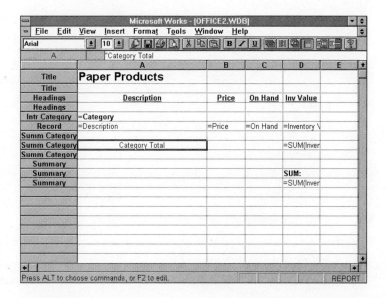

When you preview the report, it should look similar to the following illustration.

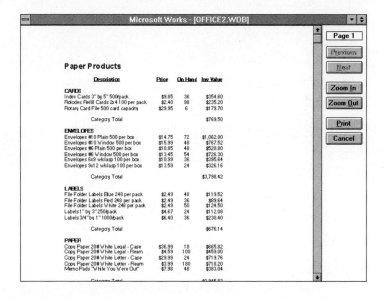

6 Save OFFICE2.WDB.

For more information on	See
Creating a standard report	Lesson 11
Sorting and grouping field entries	Lesson 11
Inserting rows	Lesson 11
Modifying titles, headings, labels, and report instructions	Lesson 11
Formatting a database report	Lesson 11

Step 5: Print Database Information

In this step, you'll change margin settings, create a footer, print the report, print a record in form view, and print records in list view.

Change margin settings

1   Open the Page Setup dialog box.

2   Change the top and bottom margins to .75 inches.

3   Change the left margin to 1.75 inches.

4   Change the right margin to 2 inches.

Create a footer

1   Open the Headers And Footers dialog box.

2   Create a footer that prints the current date, left-aligned, and the current time, right-aligned.

Print a report

1   Click the Print button on the toolbar.

2   Switch to list view and show all records.

Print a record in form view

1   Change to form view.

2   Display a record you want to print.

3   Open the Print dialog box and select only the current record for printing.

4   Click OK to print the record.

Print records in list view

1   Change to list view.

2   Hide records 12 through 17.

3   Show the hidden records.

4   Open the Page Setup dialog box and change the orientation to Landscape.

5   Click the Print button on the toolbar.

6   Show all records.

7   Save your work.

For more information on	See
Changing margin settings	Lesson 9 Lesson 11
Creating headers and footers	Lesson 11
Printing a report	Lesson 11
Printing records in form view	Lesson 9
Printing records in list view	Lesson 9

If You Want to Continue to the Next Lesson

1   Double-click the Document Control-menu box in the menu bar.

2   Be sure the Startup dialog box is open.

If You Want to Quit Works for Now

▶   Double-click the Application Control-menu box in the Microsoft Works title bar.

4 Using Communications

Getting Started with Communications

Important   In order to complete the exercises in this lesson, you'll need a modem and access to an information service, a bulletin board, or a friend's computer that has communication capabilities. (For more information about these services, see the section "Starting a Communications Session.")

The standard devices people use to communicate with others and receive information are telephones, newspapers, radios, and televisions. With the Works Communications tool and a modem (a device that your computer uses to send and receive information over telephone lines), you can have another, often more efficient method of exchanging information. Using your computer, you can quickly send and receive short messages or large documents to people in the next office or even in another city. You can use your computer to connect to online information services for the latest news, sports, medical, legal, and other information. Using special-interest computer bulletin boards and computer services, you can buy and sell stock, make travel reservations, or shop for your favorite products without leaving the comfort of your home or office.

At West Coast Sales, the Communications tool is often used to share information electronically between stores and affiliates. When the spring video promotion is over, you will electronically send various reports about the results of the sale to the main West Coast Sales branch office. Before you can send your information, you'll need to learn how to use the Works Communications tool.

In this lesson, you'll learn the basics of using the Communications tool, including how to connect to another computer and how to send and receive information.

If your screen does not match the illustrations in this lesson, see the Appendix, "Matching the Exercises."

You will learn how to:

- Start and quit a Communications session.
- Connect and reconnect to another computer.
- Send and receive files.
- Record and play back scripts.

Estimated lesson time: 20 minutes

Start the lesson

For information about changing settings, see the Microsoft Works User's Guide, *Chapter 8, "Changing communication settings."*

Note   Before you start this lesson, you might find it helpful to contact a friend or associate whose computer has communications capabilities and ask him or her to work through the exercises with you.

▶ Make sure your computer's settings are compatible with the computer you want to connect to. If the settings are not compatible, you should change them prior to starting this exercise.

Starting a Communications Session

Using your computer to communicate with another computer is similar to talking on the telephone—you dial a number, make a connection, and have a conversation. However, instead of using your voice, you communicate by typing and reading text on the screen, exchanging documents, or selecting menu options to view information. You can use the Communications tool to make computer-to-computer connections to online information services, bulletin boards, or co-workers' computers.

An online information service provides information and usually allows you to interact with that information. For example, a service might provide airline schedules and allow you to make travel reservations. Some popular information services include CompuServe, Prodigy, GEnie, and America Online. Before you can connect or "sign on" to an information service, you need to obtain an account or subscription. The service will then provide you with a phone number, communications settings, and sign-on/sign-off procedures. You can find starter kits for many services at your local computer software store.

Bulletin boards are usually smaller local services that you can use to exchange information about a specific subject. Many bulletin boards are affiliated with computer magazines and newspapers or local computer clubs. Before you can connect to a bulletin board, you need to contact the organization that operates the bulletin board and obtain such information as the telephone number, communications settings, a password, and sign-on/sign-off procedures.

You might connect to the computer of a friend or business associate if you need to transfer a file from your computer to theirs or if you want to have an electronic conversation. Before you can make this type of connection, you must make sure that both computers have compatible communications applications and you must know the telephone number of the other computer.

In the next exercises, you'll connect to another computer for the first time, quit a communications session, save a communications document, and reconnect to the other computer.

Note   Before you start the next exercises, be sure you have the phone number of an information service, bulletin board, or an associate's computer and that the other computer is ready to answer your call.

Connect to another computer for the first time

Before you can communicate or exchange information with another computer, both computers must be set up to follow the same rules, or *settings*. Works uses the standard settings used by most services.

Communications

1   In the Startup dialog box, click the Communications button.

Works opens a new Communications document and displays the Easy Connect dialog box.

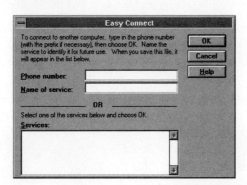

2   In the Phone Number text box, type the number of the computer to which you want to connect.

You can include a prefix or area code in the number, for example 1-500-555-4567. Hyphens are optional.

Tip   Insert commas in a phone number when you need a pause during dialing. For example, to dial 9 for an outside line and pause before dialing a number, type 9,555-4567. If you need a longer pause, use two or more commas.

---

3   In the Name Of Service text box, type **SBS Connection**

It's a good practice to type the name of the service, bulletin board, or person you are calling. The name will later appear on the Phone menu and in the Easy Connect dialog box so you can quickly reconnect to the other computer.

4   Click the OK button.

Works dials the number and displays the Dial Status dialog box, which tracks the progress of the connection operation.

Important   If Works cannot make a connection, it displays a message box indicating the nature of the problem. For example, the communications settings might be incorrect or your modem might not be connected properly. You'll need to rectify the problem before you can make a connection.

---

5 When the other computer responds, type your password, identification number, or other sign-on information, if required.

If you connected to an information service or bulletin board, you might see a menu or other instructions on your screen. If you connected to an associate's computer, you might see a greeting.

6 If you've connected to an associate's computer, type a short greeting informing the other person that you are in the process of learning how to use the Works Communications tool.

Quit a communications session

When you are finished communicating with another computer, you need to sign off and disconnect from that computer.

1 If you are connected to an information service or bulletin board, perform the required steps to properly sign off from the other computer.

Important Always sign off from an information service or bulletin board before you disconnect or you might receive unnecessary phone charges for the time it takes the service to recognize that you have disconnected.

Dial/HangUp

2 Click the Dial/HangUp button on the toolbar.

3 Click the OK button.

Save a Communications document

When you connect to another computer, Works creates a Communications document that contains the information necessary to make the connection. You can save this document and open it during a later session to load the phone number and sign-on procedures.

1 From the File menu, choose Save As.

The Save As dialog box appears.

2 In the File Name text box, type **connect1**

3 In the Directories list box, double-click the WORKSSBS folder icon.

The Save As dialog box should now match the following illustration.

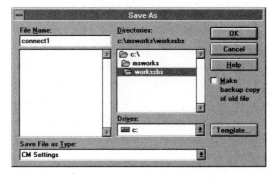

4 Click the OK button.

Works saves the Communications document with the extension WCM.

Reconnect to another computer

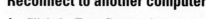

Easy Connect

1 Click the Easy Connect button on the toolbar.

The Easy Connect dialog box appears, listing the names of the eight most recently used services.

Note If you want to reconnect to a service that is not listed in the Easy Connect dialog box, you must choose Open Existing File from the File menu and then select the name of the file in the Open dialog box.

---

2 In the Services list box, double-click SBS Connection.

A message box appears asking if you want to connect to the other computer.

3 Click the OK button.

Works dials the number and displays the Dial Status dialog box to inform you of the progress of the connection operation.

Dial/HangUp

Tip You can click the Dial/Hangup button on the toolbar to quickly dial the phone number of the last service to which you were connected.

---

4 When the other computer responds, type your password, identification number, or other sign-on information, if required.

Tip If you get a busy signal or if the other computer doesn't respond, you can choose Dial Again from the Phone menu to quickly redial the last number.

---

5 When you are finished communicating with the other computer, perform the required sign-off procedures.

6 Click the Dial/Hangup button and then click the OK button.

Dial/HangUp

Transferring Files

When you connect to another computer, there are two ways you can send and receive information: You can type or copy text to the screen and send that text to the other computer or you can transfer an entire file.

When you transfer a file from your computer to another one, the other computer saves the file on its disk. When you receive a file from another computer (sometimes called *downloading*), the file is saved on your disk. If you have trouble getting the other computer to respond to your commands, you can send a break signal to get its attention. Sending a break signal is similar to asking a telephone operator to break in on a telephone conversation.

In the next exercises, you'll transfer files.

Note   Before you start the next exercises, be sure you have the phone number of an information service, bulletin board, or an associate's computer and that the other computer user is prepared to send and receive files.

Send a file

1   Connect to the computer to which you will send the file.

2   Ask the other computer user what transfer protocol they are using, if necessary.

Transfer Settings

3   Click the Transfer Settings button on the toolbar.

The Settings dialog box appears showing the Transfer settings.

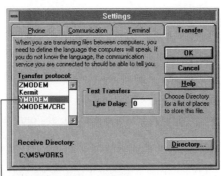

*Select the transfer protocol
the other computer is using*

4   Select the same transfer protocol the other computer is using and then click the OK button.

Note   You can send an ASCII text file or a binary file to another computer. An ASCII text file is one containing only text and no formatting; a binary file is a formatted file, such as a Works document. Select the Text option if you are sending a text file or the Binary option if you are sending a Works document or other formatted file for use with another application.

5   From the Tools menu, choose Send File.

The Send File dialog box appears.

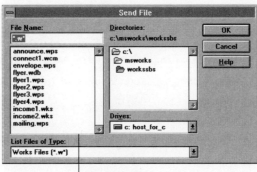

Select the file
you want to send

6   In the Directories list box, double-click the WORKSSBS folder icon if it is not already open.

If the other computer is not responding to your commands, you can send a break signal to get its attention by choosing Break from the Phone menu.

7   In the File Name list box, select ANNOUNCE.WPS.

8   Click the OK button.

Works begins sending the file to the other computer and indicates the progress of the transfer. You can press ESC if you want to cancel a file transfer before it is completed.

9   After the file transfer is completed, perform the required sign-off procedures.

10   Click the Dial/Hangup button on the toolbar to disconnect from the other computer.

Dial/HangUp

Receive a file

1   Connect to the computer from which you will receive the file.

2   Be sure the other computer is using the same transfer protocol you are using.

3   Ask the other computer user to send the file to your computer.

4   From the Tools menu, choose Receive File.

The Receive File dialog box appears.

5   In the Directories list box, double-click the WORKSSBS folder icon if it is not already open.

6 If you are using the Xmodem protocol, type **receive1** in the File Name text box.

Note If you are using the Ymodem, Zmodem, or Kermit protocol, you must receive the file with its original name. Works will transfer the file without displaying the Receive File dialog box.

---

7 Click the OK button.

Works begins transferring the file to your computer and indicates the progress of the transfer.

If the information the other computer is sending is scrolling on your screen faster than you can read it, you can click the Pause button on the toolbar to temporarily halt the file transfer. To resume the file transfer, click the Pause button again.

Pause

8 After the file transfer is completed, perform the required sign-off procedures.

9 Click the Dial/Hangup button on the toolbar to disconnect from the other computer.

Dial/HangUp

10 In the Communications document window, double-click the Control-menu box.

The Communications document closes and the Startup dialog box appears.

Automating Connections

You can use *scripts*, which are recorded sequences of keystrokes and commands, to automate repetitive or lengthy communication tasks. After you record a script, you can play it back and Works will automatically perform the series of tasks you recorded.

You can record *sign-on scripts*, which automate the steps you take to sign on to a service, or *other scripts*, which automate tasks you perform after you sign on to a service, such as navigating through a series of menus to access a particular section of an information service.

In the next exercises, you'll record a sign-on script, record a script for other tasks, and play back a script.

Record a sign-on script

Before you can record a sign-on script, you must have already saved a Communications document that connects you to the service for which you want to record the sign-on script.

1 Under Recently Used Files, double-click CONNECT1.WCM to open the document.

2 Click the OK button to connect to the other computer.

3 After you are connected to the other computer, choose Record Script from the Tools menu.

The Record Script dialog box appears.

4 Under Type Of Script, select Sign-on, and then click the OK button.

The text "Recording a script" appears in the status bar.

5 Perform the procedures required to sign on to the computer or service.

Works records your entries and the other computer's responses.

6 From the Tools menu, choose End Recording.

Save

7 Click the Save button on the toolbar.

The sign-on script is saved with the document. The next time you open the CONNECT1.WCM document, Works will automatically connect and sign on to the other computer.

Record a script for other tasks

After you connect and sign on to a computer or service, you can record scripts that automate other tasks.

1 From the Tools menu, choose Record Script.

2 Under Type Of Script, select Other.

3 In the Script Name text box, type **Test Script**

A script name can contain as many as 15 characters, including spaces.

4 Click the OK button.

The text "Recording a script" appears in the status bar.

5 Perform any sequence of steps, such as typing your logon name and password or selecting a series of menu items.

Works records your actions and the other computer's responses.

6 From the Tools menu, choose End Recording.

Save

7 Click the Save button on the toolbar.

The script is saved with the CONNECT1.WCM document.

8 Perform the required sign-off procedures.

9 Click the Dial/Hangup button on the toolbar to disconnect from the other computer.

Dial/HangUp

10 In the Communications document window, double-click the Control-menu box to close CONNECT1.WCM.

Play back a script

1 From the Startup dialog box, open CONNECT1.WCM.

2 Click the OK button to connect to the other computer.

Works automatically plays back the sign-on script and signs on to the computer or service.

3 On the menu bar, choose Tools.

A list of available scripts appears on the Tools menu.

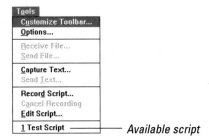

——— *Available script*

4 Choose 1 Test Script.

Works plays back the sequence of keystrokes and commands recorded in the script.

5 Perform the required sign-off procedures.

6 Click the Dial/Hangup button on the toolbar to disconnect from the other computer.

7 In the Communications document window, double-click the Control-menu box to close CONNECT1.WCM.

Dial/HangUp

One Step Further

The text you receive during a Communications session appears in the active Communications document window. However, the document window is only a temporary holding area, called a *buffer*. When you save and close the Communications document, the settings are saved, but the text in the document window is lost.

The buffer can hold as many as 256,000 lines of text. If you expect to receive more text than the buffer can hold, or if you just want to keep the information you receive in a file, you can save all of the text that appears on your screen in a file as it is received. In the next exercise, you'll capture incoming text in a file.

Capture incoming text in a file

1 Connect to the computer from which you want to receive text.

2 Ask the other computer user to start sending text.

Capture Text

3 Click the Capture Text button on the toolbar.

The Capture Text dialog box appears.

4 In the File Name text box, type **capture1.txt**

Note   You can type any descriptive filename for the text you want to capture. For example, if the other computer user is sending you the text of an article about country homes in England, you might type the filename BRITHOME.TXT.

---

5 In the Directories list box, double-click the WORKSSBS folder icon.

The Capture Text dialog box should now match the following illustration.

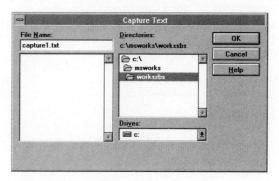

6 Click the OK button.

Works captures all incoming text during the Communications session, creates the specified file, and places the captured text in the file in the WORKSSBS directory.

Note   If the file you specify already exists in the selected directory, Works displays a dialog box with three options. You can click the Append button to add the incoming text to the end of the existing file, you can click the Replace button to replace the contents of the existing file with the incoming text, or you can click the Cancel button to return to the Capture Text dialog box, where you can type a different filename.

Capture Text

7 Click the Capture Text button on the toolbar to stop capturing text.

Tip   You can also choose End Capture Text from the Tools menu to stop capturing text.

8 Perform the required sign-off procedures.

9 Click the Dial/Hangup button on the toolbar to disconnect from the other computer.

Dial/HangUp

If You Want to Continue to the Next Lesson

1 Double-click the Document Control-menu box in the Communications document window.

2 Be sure the Startup dialog box is open.

*Document
Control-menu box*

If You Want to Quit Works for Now

▶ Double-click the Application Control-menu box in the Microsoft Works title bar.

*Application
Control-menu box*

Lesson Summary

To	Do this	Button
Connect to another computer for the first time	Click the Communications button in the Startup dialog box, type a phone number and service name in the Easy Connect dialog box, and then click the OK button. When the other computer responds, type your password, identification number, or other sign-on information.	
Quit a Communications session	Perform the steps required to sign off from the other computer, click the Dial/Hangup button on the toolbar, and then click the OK button.	
Save a Communications document	From the File menu, choose Save As, type a filename in the File Name text box, select a directory in the Directories list box, and then click the OK button.	
Reconnect to another computer	Click the Easy Connect button on the toolbar, double-click the name of the service in the Services list box, and then click the OK button. When the other computer responds, type your password, identification number, or other sign-on information.	
Send a file to another computer	Connect to the other computer and be sure both computers are using the same transfer protocol. From the Tools menu, choose Send File, select a directory and filename, and then click the OK button.	
Receive a file from another computer	Connect to the other computer and be sure both computers are using the same transfer protocol. From the Tools menu, choose Receive File, select a directory and type a filename, and then click the OK button.	

To	Do this	Button
Record a sign-on script	Connect to another computer, choose Record Script from the Tools menu, select Sign-on under Type Of Script, and then click the OK button. Perform the procedures required to sign on to the other computer or service, choose End Recording from the Tools menu, and then click the Save button on the toolbar to save the script with the Communications document.	💾
Record a script for other tasks	Connect and sign on to another computer, choose Record Script from the Tools menu, select Other under Type Of Script, type a name in the Script text box, and then click the OK button. Perform the steps you want to record, choose End Recording from the Tools menu, and then click the Save button on the toolbar to save the script with the Communications document.	💾
Play back a sign-on script	Open the Communications document that contains the script, and then click the OK button to connect to the other computer.	
Play back a named script	Choose the name of the script from the Tools menu.	
Capture incoming text to a file	Connect to another computer, click the Capture Text button on the toolbar, type a filename and select a directory in the Capture Text dialog box, and then click the OK button. When you are finished capturing text, choose End Capture Text from the Tools menu.	🔒

For more information on	See in the *Microsoft Works User's Guide*
Connecting to another computer	Chapter 8, "Making a connection over phone lines" Chapter 8, "Making a cable connection"
Transferring files	Chapter 8, "Sending text and files" Chapter 8, "Receiving and saving text and files"
Recording and playing back scripts	Chapter 8, "Recording scripts and playing them back"

For online information about	From the Help menu, choose Contents and then
Connecting to another computer	Choose "Communications," choose "Starting a communications session," and select the topic "Connecting."
Transferring files	Choose "Communications," choose "Exchanging information," and select the topic "Exchanging information overview."
Recording and playing back scripts	Choose "Communications," choose "Scripts," and select either "Recording a script" or "Playing back a script."

Review & Practice

In Part 4, "Using Communications," you learned the basics of using the Communications tool, including how to connect and reconnect to another computer, how to send and receive information, and how to record and play back scripts. If you want to practice these skills and test your understanding, you can work through the Review & Practice section following this lesson.

Part 4   Review & Practice

You can practice the skills you learned in Part 4 by working through this Review & Practice section. You will use the Communications tool to connect to another computer, send a message, reconnect to another computer, and send a file.

Scenario

The quarterly investor review meeting of West Coast Sales is scheduled for next week. You are responsible for notifying various individuals of the meeting and distributing investor information before the meeting. You'll use the Works Communications tool to connect to the computer of a new attendee and send a message notifying this individual about the meeting. Later, you'll reconnect to the same computer and send a file of investor information.

Note   Before you start this Review & Practice section, contact a friend or associate whose computer has communications capabilities and ask him or her to work through the exercises with you.

You will review and practice how to:

- Connect and communicate with another computer.
- Quit a Communications session.
- Save a Communications document.
- Reconnect and send a file to another computer.

Estimated practice time: 15 minutes

Step 1: Connect to and Communicate with Another Computer

In this step, you'll connect to another computer for the first time and send a message.

1 Open a new Communications document.

2 In the Easy Connect dialog box, type the phone number and name of the computer you are calling, and then connect to the other computer.

3 Type and send the following message to the other computer user:

   The quarterly meeting to review the status of our clients and their investments will be on Tuesday of next week. I will send you our investor information file within the next hour. Will anyone from your staff be accompanying you to the meeting?

4   Have the other computer user send you a confirmation message and reply.

For more information on	See
Connecting to another computer for the first time	Lesson 12

Step 2: Quit a Communications Session

In this step, you'll disconnect from the other computer.

1   Type a closing message to the other computer user; for example, **Goodbye**

2   Hang up and disconnect from the other computer.

For more information on	See
Quitting a Communications session	Lesson 12

Step 3: Save a Communications Document

In this step, you'll save the active Communications document.

1   Open the Save As dialog box.

2   Save the Communications document as CONNECT2.WCM in the C:\MSWORKS\WORKSSBS directory.

For more information on	See
Saving a Communications document	Lesson 12

Step 4: Reconnect and Send a File to another Computer

In this step, you'll reconnect and send a file to the other computer.

1   Open the Easy Connect dialog box.

2   Reconnect to the same computer you connected to in Step 1.

3   Be sure you are using the same transfer protocol the other computer is using.

4   Send the file INVESTOR.WDB to the other computer.

5   After the file transfer is completed, disconnect from the other computer.

For more information on	See
Sending a file	Lesson 12

If You Want to Quit Works for Now

1 Click the Save button on the toolbar.

2 Double-click the Application Control-menu box in the Microsoft Works title bar.

Appendix

Matching the Exercises

There are several settings available within Microsoft Works for Windows that can change how some screens appear as well as the how certain features operate. If you or another person have changed these settings, your screens may appear different than those shown in this book. If your screens do not match the illustrations in the lessons or if you are not able to produce the same results presented in the exercises, you can check this appendix to determine if the settings on your computer differ from those used in this book, and if so, how to change them to match the exercises.

Using the Practice Files

At the beginning of most lessons, you open files or sample documents that are contained on the Practice Files diskette. These files should be installed into a subdirectory called WORKSSBS located in the MSWORKS directory. The instructions for installing the exercise files are in the "Getting Ready" section.

Matching Your Screen Display to the Illustrations

The settings used in this book are, for the most part, the defaults that were preset when you installed Microsoft Works for Windows. Within each of the Works for Windows programs, you can change the appearance of your screen by turning different options on or off. The following sections describe steps that you can complete for each of the programs so that you can complete the exercises and match your screen display to the illustrations in the book.

Display the default toolbar

If you or another person have been using Works for Windows prior to using this book, you may have turned off the toolbars to show as much text as possible on the screen. If your toolbar does not appear at the top of the screen, you should turn it on and make sure Tool Tips is enabled. When Tool Tips is enabled, a descriptive label appears whenever you position the mouse pointer over a toolbar button.

Word Processor

1   In the Startup dialog box, click the Word Processor button.

2   From the View menu, click the Toolbar option to activate it if it isn't already activated.

Note   When a menu command is activated, a check mark appears to the left of the command name. A command that does not have a check mark next to it is not activated. You activate or deactivate a command by clicking it.

---

3   From the Tools menu, choose Customize Toolbar.

The Customize Works Toolbar dialog box appears.

4 Click the Reset button.

5 Turn on the Enable Tool Tips check box and then click the OK button.

Set display options

To ensure that you will be able to complete the exercises and match the illustrations in this book, you should make sure the following display options are in effect: Show Status Bar, Use 3-D Dialogs, Drag And Drop, and Helpful Mouse Pointers.

The Show Status Bar option makes the status bar visible on your screen. To complete some of the exercise steps, you will need to access the status bar. The Use 3-D Dialogs option makes dialog boxes appear with a three-dimensional effect. This effect makes the dialog boxes visually appealing, but does not affect how they function. If this option is not in effect, your dialog boxes will look different than those shown in the book, but they will still operate correctly. The Drag And Drop option enables you to use the drag-and-drop feature, which you will need to use to complete some of the exercises. The Helpful Mouse Pointers option enables the mouse pointer to change shape to indicate actions you can perform at any given time.

1 From the Tools menu, choose Options.

The Options dialog box appears.

2 Turn on the Show Status Bar check box.

3 Turn on the Use 3-D Dialogs check box.

4 Turn on the Drag And Drop check box.

5 Turn on the Helpful Mouse Pointers check box.

Your Options dialog box should match the following illustration.

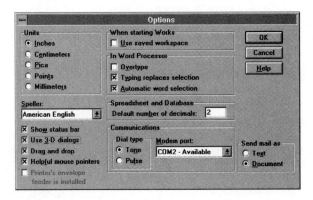

6 Click the OK button.

Hide the Cue Cards

Cue Cards are brief instructions that appear on your screen to help you complete tasks. To complete the exercises in this book, you should turn off the display of the Cue Cards so that you can see more of the documents.

▶ From the Help menu, deactivate the Cue Cards option.

Use the default page setup

Most of the exercises within this book use the default page margin, size, and orientation settings. If your settings do not match the default settings, you can reset them.

1 From the File menu, choose Page Setup.

2 Click the Margins tab and then click the Reset button.

Your screen should match the following illustration.

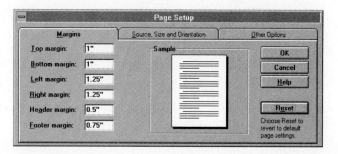

3 Click the Source, Size And Orientation tab and then click the Reset button.

Your screen should match the following illustration.

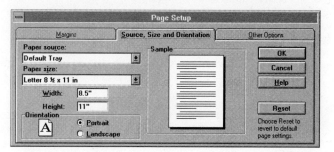

4 Click the Other Options tab and then click the Reset button.

Your screen should match the following illustration.

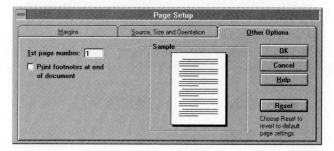

5 Click the OK button.

Matching the Word Processor Options

In order for you to successfully complete the exercises in the Word Processor lessons, the following options need to be in effect.

Display the ruler

The ruler serves as a guide for aligning text within documents. The ruler is not required in all of the lessons, but the illustrations in the book show the ruler displayed. You should display the ruler to match the illustrations.

▶ From the View menu, activate the Ruler option.

Match the character display

Works can display symbols or codes for all of the characters in a document. For example, Works can display paragraph symbols at the end of each paragraph. To make the screens more readable, you should make sure this option is not in effect

▶ From the View menu, deactivate the All Characters option.

Match the word wrap display

You can make Works wrap paragraphs of text within the display area of your screen regardless of the page margins and orientation. This is useful if you are doing a lot of typing of text prior to formatting it. For the illustrations in this book, the Wrap For Windows option is not in effect.

▶ From the View menu, deactivate the Wrap For Windows option.

Set spelling options

If the Always Suggest option is in effect, Works will automatically offer suggestions for words it does not recognize during a spelling check. By default, this option is not in effect. If you have been using Works for a while, you may have decided to use the Always Suggest option.

1   Type ASDF in a Word Processor document and then position the insertion point at the beginning of the document.

2   From the Tools menu, choose Spelling.

    The Spelling dialog box appears.

3   Turn off the Always Suggest check box.

4   Click the Cancel button.

5   From the File menu, choose Close.

6   Do not save the changes to the Word Processor document.

    The Startup dialog box should now appear.

Matching the Spreadsheet Options

In order for you to successfully complete the exercises in the Spreadsheet lessons, the following options need to be in effect.

Show the gridlines

By default, Works displays gridlines between each row and column in the spreadsheet window. You can turn off the gridlines to improve the appearance of a spreadsheet on the screen. Turning the gridlines on or off does not affect how the spreadsheet will print. In the Spreadsheet lessons, the gridlines are turned on.

Spreadsheet

1   In the Startup dialog box, click the Spreadsheet button.

2   From the View menu, activate the Gridlines option.

Use the default page setup

Although you reset the page setup options for the Word Processor, you must reset the Other Options settings again for the Spreadsheet.

1   From the File menu, choose Page Setup.

2   Click the Other Options tab and then click the Reset button.

Your screen should match the following illustration.

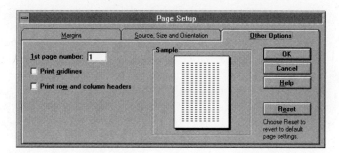

3   Click the OK button.

4   From the File menu, choose Close.

5   Do not save changes if you are prompted to do so.

Matching the Database Options

In order for you to successfully complete the exercises in the Database lessons, the following options need to be in effect.

Show the field lines

By default, Works displays lines between each row and column in the database list window. You can turn off the form lines to improve the appearance of a database on the screen. Turning the form lines on or off does not affect how the database will print or appear in form view. In the Database lessons, the form lines are turned on.

1   In the Startup dialog box, click the Database button.

2   From the View menu, activate the Field Lines option.

Database

Use the grid to align items on the form

When you are designing a database form, you can use a grid to align items either horizontally or vertically. Most of the exercises do not require you to use the grid, but it will make matching the alignment of items on your screen with the illustrations easier.

▶   From the Format menu, activate the Snap To Grid option.

Use the default page setup

Although you reset the page setup options for the Word Processor, you must reset the Other Options settings again for the Database.

1   From the File menu, choose Page Setup.

2   Click the Other Options tab and then click the Reset button.

Your screen should match the following illustration.

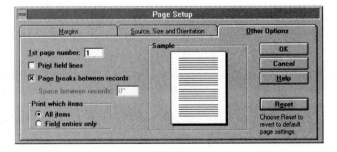

3   Click the OK button.

4   From the File menu, choose Close.

5   Do not save changes if you are prompted to do so.

Glossary

active   An application window or document that you are currently using or working on. You can have several application windows and documents open at the same time, but only one of them can be active at any given time.

alignment   In a Word Processor document, the horizontal position of text between the left and right margins. In a Spreadsheet or Database document, alignment refers to the horizontal position of information within cells or fields.

application window   A window that contains an open application, such as the Word Processor tool or the Spreadsheet tool. The application window provides the space in which you work on a document, and it displays the menu bar and the toolbar.

argument   Numbers, cell references, or text that you enter into functions to make calculations.

ASCII   An acronym for American Standard Code for Information Interchange. ASCII is a standard file format that can be used by most applications. Documents stored in ASCII format contain only unformatted text and numbers.

AutoStart templates   Predefined templates that are installed when you run the Works Setup program.

best fit   A Works feature that automatically adjusts the size of a spreadsheet column or database field to accommodate the width of the longest entry.

binary file   Any file that is not an ASCII text file.

borders   Lines and boxes that you place around paragraphs, cells, fields, or drawing objects. You can use borders to draw attention to important information or to separate sections of a document.

break signal   An attention signal you can send to another computer during a Communications session if it is not responding to your commands.

buffer   A temporary storage area for information sent and received during a Communications session. The buffer can store as many as 256,000 lines of text.

bulletin board   An electronic communications system that stores and distributes messages, files, and programs. When you connect to a bulletin board system (BBS), you can communicate with other users, upload information from your computer to the BBS, and view and download information from the BBS to your computer.

button   An on-screen symbol that represents a Works operation or command. You click a button to execute its corresponding command.

calculation formula   An entry in a database report definition used to perform a calculation on field entries.

category labels   Text that identifies each category on the X-axis in a chart.

cell   The area formed by the intersection of a column and a row in a spreadsheet.

cell reference   The location of a cell in a spreadsheet, identified by the column label and row number. For example, the intersection of the second column and the fifth row is cell B5.

chart   A visual representation of spreadsheet data.

click   To position the mouse pointer over an object on the screen and quickly press and release a mouse button.

clip art   Ready-made graphics that you can insert in documents. You use the ClipArt Gallery to view and select clip art.

Clipboard   An area in computer memory where information is temporarily stored after being cut or copied from a document. You can paste the contents of the Clipboard into the same Works document, into a different Works document, or into a document in another Windows-based application.

close   To exit an application or document and remove its window from the screen.

column labels   The letters that appear at the top of each column in a spreadsheet.

conditions   Components of a query that specify the parameters of the query. For example, the query "which people are named Smith and have blue eyes and brown hair" has three conditions. A condition can also be called a *criteria* or *query sentence*.

connect   To establish communication with another computer.

Control menu   A menu containing commands that you can choose to move, resize, and close the active window.

Control-menu box   The rectangular button in the upper left corner of a window or dialog box that you click to open the Control menu.

criteria   *See* conditions.

Cue Cards   Instructions for basic tasks that appear in a window next to the active document.

cursor   *See* insertion point.

database   An organized collection of information.

database form   A form that you use to enter information into a database.

data labels   Text or numbers from spreadsheet cells that are displayed next to or above the bars, lines, or markers in a chart.

dialog box   A pop-up window of options that appears when you choose a menu command followed by an ellipsis (...).

directory   A separate area on a disk in which you store a group of files. For example, you might store all of the Word Processor and Spreadsheet files you use to create management reports in a directory named REPORTS.

disconnect   To break a communication connection with another computer.

document window   A window within an application window in which you create or modify a document.

double-click   To click a mouse button twice in rapid succession. You double-click to perform tasks such as opening a document, selecting text, or closing a window.

download   To receive a file or other information from another computer user, information service, or bulletin board system.

drag   To hold down a mouse button, move the mouse pointer to a different position, and then release the mouse button. You drag when you want to highlight information or move an object or window.

drag-and-drop   A technique you can use to move or copy highlighted information with the mouse. To move, drag the highlighted information to a new position. To copy, hold down CTRL and drag the highlighted information to a new position.

field   A category of information in a database, such as telephone numbers.

field entry instruction   An entry in a database report definition that specifies inclusion of the entries from a specific field in the report.

field name   A name that identifies a database field and the type of information it contains.

file   A collection of information stored on a disk under an identifying name. A file can contain an application or a document.

fill palette   In Microsoft Draw, the area at the bottom of the drawing window that contains color boxes you can click to change the fill color of an object.

font   A set of characters with a specific design and a similar appearance. Each font has its own name, such as Arial or Times New Roman.

font size   The size of the characters in a font. Font size is usually measured in points, with one point equal to approximately 1/72 inch.

font style   The appearance of the characters in a font. You can apply font styles such as bold, underline, and italic.

footer   Information that prints at the bottom of every document page. You can use footers to add page numbers, report titles, dates, and other repetitive information to documents.

formatting   Tasks that affect the appearance of a document, such as changing margins, applying a new font, or adding headers and footers.

formula   An entry in a spreadsheet cell or database field that performs a calculation using existing values in other spreadsheet cells or database fields.

formula bar   In a Spreadsheet or Database document, the area below the toolbar that displays the contents of the highlighted cell or field. You can use the formula bar to edit cell and field entries.

form view   The database view in which records appear on a database form and can be viewed only one at a time.

function   A predefined formula that performs special or advanced calculations in a spreadsheet or database.

gridlines   Horizontal and vertical lines between rows and columns in a spreadsheet or database. In a chart, the lines between categories or intervals on an axis.

handles   Small squares that appear on the borders of a highlighted field or other object. You can drag a handle to resize or move the field or object.

header   Information that prints at the top of every document page. You can use headers to add page numbers, report titles, dates, and other repetitive information to documents.

highlight   To mark text, cells, or fields that you want to modify, move, or copy. When you highlight information, it appears in reverse video (light text on a dark background) on the screen. When you highlight a single spreadsheet cell or database field, a dark border appears around the cell or field.

icon   An on-screen symbol that represents a disk drive, directory, application, document, or other object that you can select and open.

indent   The distance between a paragraph and the left and right margins in a Word Processor document.

information service   An electronic communications system that stores information you can view and download to your computer.

insertion point   A blinking vertical bar that shows you where text or objects will appear on the screen or where an action, such as searching for text in a document, will begin.

label Descriptive text that appears in every record on a database form.

leader characters Characters that appear between tab stops in a table. You can display leader characters as dots, dashes, double-dashes, or underlines.

legend Text and symbols that identify the markers, colors, and patterns that represent Y-series values in a chart.

line palette In Microsoft Draw, the area at the bottom of the drawing window that contains color boxes you can click to change the line color of an object.

line spacing The amount of space between each line in a paragraph.

list box An area in a dialog box that contains a list of items for selection.

list view The database view in which you can view several records at one time. The records appear in table format.

lock An action that prevents the contents of spreadsheet cells and database fields from being altered.

menu A list of commands that you can execute with a keystroke or by clicking the mouse.

menu bar The horizontal bar near the top of an application window that contains the names of menus.

modem A device that allows two computers to communicate via telephone lines.

number format A setting that specifies how numbers will appear in spreadsheet cells or database fields. You can display numbers as percentages or with currency symbols or commas.

object Any piece of data in a document, such as a graphics image or a text selection.

open To start an application, display the contents of a document in a window, or enlarge a minimized window.

orientation The position of a document on the page. Orientation can be portrait (vertical) or landscape (horizontal).

pagination A feature that updates and adjusts the page breaks in a document.

palette *See* fill palette *and* line palette

paragraph spacing The amount of space above and below a paragraph.

placeholder An object that indicates where information from another document will be inserted into the current document. For example, you might have a placeholder in a Word Processor document to insert information from a field in a Database document.

point   *See* font size.

print merge   A feature that lets you combine multiple sources of text into a single document, such as a form letter, mailing label, or envelope.

program group window   A window that contains one or more program icons that you can double-click to open applications.

protection   A feature that you use to prevent alteration of spreadsheet cells, database fields, or form designs.

query   A question you ask about the information stored in a database, such as "which people live in the state of California." When you apply a query, Works displays all of the records that match the correct answer to your question.

query sentence   *See* conditions.

query view   The database view in which you can specify more than three conditions and use formulas and functions.

range   A block of cells in a spreadsheet. A range can be as small as a single cell or as large as an entire spreadsheet.

range reference   The location of a block of cells in a spreadsheet, identified by the cell reference of the first and last cells in the range, separated by a colon; for example B5:E21.

record   A collection of related information in a database about a person, a place, an item, or an event. For example, the name, address, and telephone number of one person is a record.

report view   The database view in which you specify how Works summarizes and prints database information.

row numbers   The numbers that appear at the beginning of each row in a spreadsheet.

ruler   A reference tool that appears near the top of a Word Processor document. You can use the ruler to quickly change the indents and tab settings for the current paragraph.

save   To store the contents of a document in a file on a disk.

script   A recorded sequence of keystrokes and commands that automates a communication task.

scroll bars   The bars located at the right and bottom edges of a window, which you can use to scroll through the window using a mouse. Each bar contains scroll arrows, which you can click to scroll one line, column, or row at a time.

search characters   Characters that specify an entry you want to search for using the find feature.

series   A range of spreadsheet information displayed in a chart. A Y-series is a range of numbers displayed as lines or bars; an X-series is a range of text entries used to identify groups or categories of data.

settings   A set of procedures that two computers use when communicating. When you send and receive files, both computers must use the same protocol.

sign off   To type the information required to disconnect from an information service or bulletin board system.

sign on   To complete a connection to an information service or bulletin board system by typing a user ID, password, or other required information.

sizing handles   *See* handles.

sort   To arrange data in a specified order. For example, you might sort a list of names and addresses into alphabetical order by last name.

spreadsheet   A grid of 256 columns and 16,384 rows in which you enter text, numbers, and formulas.

standard report   A database report that contains a report title, the fields you specify, and report statistics.

synonym   A word with the same or nearly the same meaning as another word. You can use the Works Thesaurus to look up synonyms and replace words in a document.

template   A predesigned document with the basic layout, formatting, and sample text already in place. You can use a template as a model for creating a new document.

toolbar   A row of buttons that appears near the top of an application window and provides shortcuts for performing common tasks.

toolbox   In Microsoft Draw, a set of nine tools on the left side of the drawing window that you can use to draw shapes and lines, add text, and view different parts of a drawing.

upload   To send information to another computer user, information service, or bulletin board system.

wildcard character   A single character used in place of a character or a group of characters in search text.

window   A rectangular area on the screen in which you can display and work with documents.

Windows-based application   An application designed to run with Microsoft Windows, which has such standard features as a menu bar, menus, and dialog boxes.

WordArt   An accessory you can use to create text objects with special effects.

wordwrap   A feature that automatically begins a new line of text when the current line reaches the right margin in a Word Processor document or a Database field.

WorksWizard   An automated process for creating documents and performing other tasks, such as copying and moving files. When you use a WorksWizard, you answer questions about the task you want to accomplish and the WorksWizard performs the task according to your specifications.

X-axis   The horizontal reference line at the bottom of a chart that identifies the categories being measured.

Y-axis   The vertical reference line on the left side of a chart that shows the units in which categories are being measured.

Index

Special Characters

... (ellipsis), xx, xxi
? (question mark as wildcard character), 194
- (subtraction operator), 84, 165
( ) (parentheses), 86
+ (addition operator), 84, 165
* (asterisk as multiplication operator), 84, 165
* (asterisk as wildcard character), 194, 204
/ (division operator), 84, 165
= (equal sign), 84, 86, 165
3-D Line Chart button, 130
3-D Line dialog box, 130

A

Add Clipart dialog box, 62–63
aligning
    cell entries, 107
    field entries, 175–76
    multiple paragraphs, 21–22
    single paragraphs, 22
Alignment command, 107, 175, 224, 225
Alignment dialog box, 107, 175, 224–25
All Characters command, 270
ALT key, xix, xx, xxii
Application Control-menu box, 4
arguments, 86
AutoStart templates
    defined, 139
    entering information in, 141–42
    opening, 139–140
    previewing, 142
    sample text, 140
    saving as documents, 142
Autosum button, 86
AVG function, 86

B

BACKSPACE key, 7
bar charts
    adding series, 121–22
    changing colors, 134

bar charts, *continued*
    changing fill patterns, 134
    creating, 120–21
best fit, 105, 172
Bold button, 28
Bold command, 61
Border command, 31, 109, 178
Border dialog box, 31–32, 109, 178
borders
    adding to cells, 109–10
    adding to fields, 178
    adding to paragraphs, 31–32
break signal, 252
buffer, 256
bulletin boards, 248
bullets
    adding, 23
    removing, 24
Bullets button, 23

C

Capture text button, 256
Capture text dialog box, 256–57
category labels, adding to charts, 123–24
cell entries
    changing number formats of, 105–6
    changing the alignment of, 107
    clearing, 89
    copying, 90
    editing, 89
    finding, 93
    moving, 91
    replacing, 88, 93
cell protection
    turning on, 113
    unlocking cells, 112–13
cell references, 79
cells
    adding borders to, 109–10
    adding shading to, 110–11
    defined, 79
    formatting, 105–11
    highlighting, 83

Train Yourself
With *Step by Step* books from Microsoft Press

The *Step by Step* books are the perfect self-paced training solution for Microsoft Office users. Each book comes with a disk that contains every example in the book. By using the practice files and following instructions in the book, you can "learn by doing," which means you can start applying what you've learned to business situations right away. If you're too busy to attend a class or if classroom training doesn't make sense for you or your office, you can build the computer skills you need with the *Step by Step* books from Microsoft Press.

Microsoft® Word 6 for Windows™
Step by Step
Catapult, Inc.
336 pages, softcover with one 3.5-inch disk
$29.95 ($39.95 Canada)   ISBN 1-55615-576-X

Microsoft® Excel 5 for Windows™
Step by Step
Catapult, Inc.
368 pages, softcover with one 3.5-inch disk
$29.95 ($39.95 Canada)   ISBN 1-55615-587-5

Microsoft Access® 2 for Windows™
Step by Step
Catapult, Inc.
375 pages, softcover with one 3.5-inch disk
$29.95 ($39.95 Canada)   ISBN 1-55615-593-X

Microsoft® Mail for Windows™
Step by Step
Catapult, Inc.
Versions 3.0b and later.
224 pages, softcover with one 3.5-inch disk
$24.95 ($32.95 Canada)   ISBN 1-55615-571-9

Microsoft Press

Running Microsoft® Software
with Bestselling Books

Running Microsoft® Works 3 for Windows™
JoAnne Woodcock, revised by Neil J. Salkind

Here is the book you need to get your home and business up and running with Microsoft Works 3 for Windows. Two books in one, the user's guide portion includes step-by-step tutorials, helpful screen illustrations, and dozens of examples covering all the productivity tools in Works. As a helpful reference, this book is great for quick lookups any time you're working with Works, complete descriptions of features, with clear explanations of how they work, are easy to find.

608 pages, softcover $24.95 ($33.95 Canada)   ISBN 1-55615-584-0

Running Word 6 for Windows™
Russell Borland

Master the power and features of Microsoft Word 6 for Windows with this updated edition of the bestselling guide for intermediate to advanced users. This example-rich guide contains scores of insights and tips not found in the documentation and includes in-depth, accessible coverage of Word's powerful new features.

832 pages, softcover $29.95 ($39.95 Canada)   ISBN 1-55615-574-3

Running Microsoft® Excel 5 for Windows™
The Cobb Group with Mark Dodge,
Chris Kinata, and Craig Stinson

Here's the most comprehensive and accessible book for all levels of spreadsheet users. It includes hundreds of tips and practical shortcuts for using the powerful new features of Microsoft Excel 5 for Windows. In addition to the step-by-step tutorials, straightforward examples, and expert advice, this updated edition features a new and improved format designed to help you find answers faster!

1184 pages, softcover $29.95 ($39.95 Canada)   ISBN 1-55615-585-9

Microsoft Press

The
Step
by Step
Companion Disk

The enclosed 3.5-inch disk contains timesaving, ready-to-use practice files that complement the lessons in this book. To use the practice files, you'll need the Microsoft® Windows™ operating system version 3.1 or later, MS-DOS® version 3.1 or later (MS-DOS version 5.0 or later is recommended, and Microsoft Works version 3 for Windows.

Each *Step by Step* lesson is closely integrated with the practice files on the disk. Before you begin the *Step by Step* lessons, we highly recommend that you read the "Getting Ready" section of the book and install the practice files on your hard disk. As you work through each lesson, be sure to follow the instructions for renaming the practice files so that you can go through a lesson more than once if you need to.

Please take a few moments to read the License Agreement on the previous page before using the enclosed disk.

Register Today!

Return the
Microsoft® Works 3 for Windows™
Step by Step
registration card for:

✔ a Microsoft Press® catalog

✔ exclusive offers on specially priced books

U.S. and Canada addresses only. Fill in information below and mail postage-free. Please mail only the bottom half of this page.

1-55615-645-6A   **W5K**   *Microsoft Works 3 for Windows Step by Step Owner Registration Card*

NAME

COMPANY (if applicable)

ADDRESS

CITY   STATE   ZIP

Your feedback is important to us.

Include your daytime telephone number, and we may call to find out how you use *Microsoft Works 3 for Windows Step by Step* and what we can do to make future editions even more useful. If we call you, we'll send you a **FREE GIFT** for your time!

(   )

DAYTIME TELEPHONE NUMBER

Fast, Easy Answers—
Anywhere, Anytime

Field Guide to Microsoft® Works 3 for Windows™
Carl Seichert & Chris Wood
If you're new to Microsoft Works for Windows and want
quick answers to quick questions about all the productivity tools
in Works and how they work together, this is the guide for you.
This handy guide is arranged by task and organized in easy-to-use,
easy-to-remember color-coded sections with rich cross-referencing
for easy lookup. Plus, look for the friendly guy in the pith helmet,
who leads you through from start to finish.
208 pages $9.95 ($12.95 Canada)   ISBN 1-55615-620-0

Microsoft *Press*

NO POSTAGE
NECESSARY
IF MAILED
IN THE
UNITED STATES

BUSINESS REPLY MAIL
FIRST-CLASS MAIL   PERMIT NO. 53   BOTHELL, WA

POSTAGE WILL BE PAID BY ADDRESSEE

MICROSOFT PRESS REGISTRATION
MICROSOFT WORKS 3 FOR WINDOWS
  STEP BY STEP
PO BOX 3019
BOTHELL WA   98041-9910